IB Music Revision Guide 2nd Edition

IB Music Revision Guide
2nd Edition

Everything You Need to Prepare for the Music Listening Examination (Standard and Higher Level 2016–2019)

Roger Paul

ANTHEM PRESS

Anthem Press
An imprint of Wimbledon Publishing Company
www.anthempress.com

This edition first published in UK and USA 2014 by ANTHEM PRESS
75–76 Blackfriars Road, London SE1 8HA, UK or PO Box 9779,
London SW19 7ZG, UK
and
244 Madison Ave #116, New York, NY 10016, USA

British Library Cataloguing-in-Publication Data
A catalogue record for this book is available from the British Library.

Library of Congress Cataloging-in-Publication Data
Names: Paul, Roger, 1965–
Title: IB music revision guide 2nd edition: everything you need to prepare for the music
listening examination (standard and higher level 2016-2019) /
Roger Paul.Description: London ; New York, NY : Anthem Press, 2016. |
Includes bibliographical references and index.
Identifiers: LCCN 2016029672 | ISBN 9781783085828 (pbk. : alk. paper)
Subjects: LCSH: Music–Examinations–Study guides. |
International baccalaureate–Study guides. | Music–Examinations, questions, etc. |
Musical dictation.
Classification: LCC MT9 .P387 2016 | DDC 780.76–dc23
LC record available at https://lccn.loc.gov/2016029672

ISBN-13: 978-1-78308-582-8 (Pbk)
ISBN-10: 1-78308-582-7 (Pbk)

This title is also available as an e-book.

CONTENTS

INTRODUCTION

For the Music section of the IB Diploma you have to complete the following tasks, depending on whether you are taking Higher Level (HL) or Standard Level (SL):

Higher Level – the following tasks are compulsory:

- Solo Performing (20 minutes of recordings) – 25 per cent of the total mark.
- Creating (3 pieces of work made from a combination of composing, arranging, music technology and pastiche) – 25 per cent of the total mark.
- Musical links investigation – a media script (up to 2,000 words) looking into music from two distinct cultures – 20 per cent of the total mark.
- Listening examination (2 ½ hours) – 30 per cent of the total mark.

Standard Level – students choose **one** of the following, which is worth 50 per cent of the total mark:

- Solo Performing (15 minutes of recordings).
- Creating (2 pieces of work made from a combination of composing, arranging, music technology and pastiche).
- Group Performing (20–30 minutes of recordings in front of an audience).

The remaining 50 per cent is made up of tasks common to both the Higher and Standard Level programmes:

- Musical Links investigation – a media script (up to 2,000 words) looking into music from two distinct cultures – 20 per cent of the total mark.
- Listening examination (2 hours) – 30 per cent of the total mark.

As you can see, both HL and SL students produce a Musical Links investigation and study for a Listening Paper. This book will help you prepare for the Listening Paper, which lasts 2 ½ hours for HL, 2 hours for SL. The paper is divided into 2 sections for both HL and SL. Section A is based on the Prescribed Works, Section B is based on Musical Styles and Cultures (a CD is provided).

All questions in either version of the Listening Paper are worth 20 marks. The total marks for the SL paper is 80 (20 for answering 1 question in Section A, 60 for 3 questions in Section B). The HL paper carries a total of 100 marks (40 for answering 2 questions in Section A, 60 for 3 questions in Section B). The differences between the HL and SL papers are shown in more detail below.

Higher Level

- Section A (prescribed works) – choose **either question 1 or 2**, followed by question 3, a Musical Links question on the prescribed works.
- Section B – choose **either question 4 or 5**, questions 6 and 7 are compulsory.
- 5 questions in 2½ hours (150 minutes) = 30 minutes per question.

Standard Level

- Section A (prescribed works) – choose **either question 1 or 2**. The links question on the prescribed works mentioned above is **not required** for SL candidates
- Section B – choose **either question 3 or 4**; questions 5 and 6 are compulsory.
- 4 questions in 2 hours (120 minutes) = 30 minutes per question.

The examinations take place in May for the Northern Hemisphere and November for the Southern Hemisphere. But, whenever your final term starts, try to ensure you have completed all of the coursework assignments so that you will have enough time left to revise fully for the Listening Paper.

Section A: Prescribed Works

2015–16:	*Petite messe solennelle* (1863) – Gioachino Rossini
	An American in Paris (1928) – George Gershwin
2017–19:	Brandenburg Concerto no. 2 in F major BWV1047 (c.1719–21) – J. S. Bach
	Dances of Galánta (1933) – Zoltán Kodály

The first two questions each focus on musical elements found in the individual works. All candidates choose **either question 1 or 2**. Typically, these questions ask you to discuss musical elements in each set work with reference to their historical context (e.g., 'demonstrate how Mozart's *Jupiter* Symphony is typical of the Classical period'). Question 3 is for HL candidates only and will require an exploration of musical links between the two Prescribed Works. You may take clean scores of the prescribed works into the exam so it is worth learning how to read and navigate them as this will enable you to find points to make and give precise examples to illustrate your answers, instead of having to rely on recalling large amounts of 'crammed' information. The examiners are particularly looking for:

- Valid, relevant musical observations.
- Accurately located and explained examples.
- Correct use of musical terms.

From page 11 onwards you will find analyses of the prescribed works and some practice questions for you to try.

Section B: Perception and Analysis of Musical Styles

In this section all candidates answer 3 questions from a choice of 4. The first two are taken from Western Classical music, whilst the other two feature extracts from Jazz, Pop and World music. Candidates are allowed to choose between the Western Classical questions. Western Classical in IB is 'classical' in the record shop sense, in that the questions are drawn from the Renaissance period up to the present day 'Modern' period. The titles and composers of the extracts are also usually given in the question headings.

Section B questions always ask you to 'analyse, examine and discuss in detail what you hear (or see in a given score) in this extract'. These are open-ended questions, but the examiners are looking to award marks for:

- Describing musical elements (instruments/voices, tempo, duration, melody, harmony, tonality, texture).
- Using the correct terminology when describing the musical elements.
- Outlining the structure of the music.
- Outlining the context of the music (period, date, composer, genre, purpose).

A score is usually provided for one of these questions and you are expected to refer to it in your answer. The accompanying CD tracks can be played as often as you wish (including during the 5 minutes' reading time at the start), and your school/college should provide a CD player capable of displaying minutes and seconds. This is important because it is the only way of giving precise locations for your examples when no score is provided. Notice that Section B carries more marks than the other sections. You should practise this type of question as frequently as you can, given that music extracts are so accessible nowadays. Although musical styles have distinguishing features, it is dangerous to assume that only those features will be heard. *You must write about what you actually hear, not just what you expect to hear.* Please see page 81 for an overview of the main styles and some practice questions, mark schemes and answers.

Continuous Prose or Note Form? Watch the Time

The IB guide states that in all questions you are required to 'build a case'. Whilst there is no requirement to write in continuous prose, the use of bullet points is not without risk. There is a danger that bullet points could be too brief and could lose you marks because you have not expressed the point in enough detail. Conversely some candidates get bogged down writing what to them feels like an essay, and you must also be mindful of the time. Remember you have around 30 minutes per question. How much of this is writing time? Remember that some of your time will be used up on thinking, planning, looking at scores and, in the case of Section B, listening to CD extracts. Although these extracts tend to be around 1'30"– 2'00" in length you will need to play them more than once. You must work quickly and efficiently in this exam, so I usually advise my students to:

- Briefly plan the answer – you must arrange your ideas into a logical argument, and you may still get some credit even if you run out of time.
- Write in 'detailed bullet points'. Make the point, give the precise location of your example and explain it.
- Leave gaps between your points so that they can be developed later if you suddenly think of something else you could mention that is related. This will help you to keep your answer organized.

MUSICAL TERMS AND DEVICES

This section of the guide is an introduction to the technical terms used in the IB music course. They are listed under the 'elements' of music they relate to (i.e., structure, melody, rhythm, tonality, harmony, texture, forces and context), so that in the examination you will be able to give relevant answers to whatever question is set. You would not score many marks – and waste a lot of time – if you wrote, for example, about polyphonic texture in a question asking you to comment on the use of melody.

Read these terms carefully and note which elements they are associated with. Notice that some terms can be used under more than one element: for example, 'pedal point' is both a harmonic and textural device. Refer to the Glossary at the back of the book if you are unfamiliar with any of them, and practise identifying them with both your eyes and ears, in scores and recordings.

Tip: use the word '**mostly**' to help clarify your answers. For example, melodies often have both steps and leaps, but if there are more steps, this could be described more accurately as 'mostly conjunct'.

Structure	
	• Binary (AB, AABB)
	• Ternary (ABA)
	• Rondo (ABACA, etc.)
	• Theme and variations ($A^1A^2A^3A^4$ etc.), variations on a Ground Bass
	• Sonata form (exposition/development/recapitulation)
	• Ritornello
	• Fugue
	• Songs: Strophic (same music for each verse), through-composed (ABCD, etc.), verse/bridge/chorus/middle eight/instrumental solo, 32-bar song (AABA)
	• 12-bar Blues (AAB)
	• Jazz: head arrangement (theme, improvised solos, theme)
	• Raga: alap/jor/gat/jhalla

Melody	<ul><li>Conjunct (stepwise) movement</li><li>Disjunct (angular) movement</li><li>Range of the melody (narrow/wide, interval between highest/lowest notes)</li><li>Key/scale of the melody: major/minor, modal, atonal, blues, raga, slendro, etc.</li><li>Use of chromatic notes/accidentals</li><li>Important motifs, used to build themes</li><li>Ornaments: passing notes, auxiliary notes, appoggiaturas, grace notes, trills, mordents, turns, etc.</li><li>Phrasing: regular/irregular, question and answer, long/short</li><li>Flowing or fragmented</li><li>Repetition, rising/falling sequence</li><li>Vocal melodies: word-setting (syllabic/melismatic), word-painting</li></ul>
Rhythm	<ul><li>Time signature or Metre: simple, e.g., 2, 3, 4 beats in a bar; compound, e.g., 5 or more beats in a bar</li><li>Changes of time signature or metre</li><li>The range of different note lengths used</li><li>Important rhythmic motifs or patterns in a piece</li><li>Dotted rhythms</li><li>Triplets and other unusual groupings</li><li>Syncopated or off-beat rhythms</li><li>Cross-rhythms, e.g., Hemiola</li><li>Polyrhythms</li><li>Accents</li><li>Ostinato patterns</li><li>Swing or shuffle rhythm, e.g., in Jazz or Blues</li><li>Flexible, *ad lib* patterns with no fixed metre</li></ul>
Tonality	<ul><li>Tonal: major or minor key</li><li>Functional harmony, i.e., the key is defined by clear cadences</li><li>Non-functional harmony, i.e., few/no cadences, but still uses the notes of the key</li><li>Atonal (no key)</li><li>Modal, e.g., pentatonic, Aeolian, Dorian, Phrygian, etc.</li><li>Modulations (changes of tonality/key) in the music</li></ul>

Harmony	• Triads (major/minor/diminished/augmented), root position or inverted • Diatonic (uses the notes of the key) • Chromatic (with accidentals) • Functional harmony, i.e., the key is defined by clear cadences • Non-functional harmony, i.e., few/no cadences, but still uses the notes of the key • Cadences (perfect/imperfect/plagal/interrupted) • Pedals (tonic/dominant, in the bass/inverted) • Circle of 5ths • Tierce de Picardie (minor piece ends on a tonic major chord) • 7th chords (dominant/major/minor/diminished) • Extended chords: 9th, 11th, 13th • Augmented 6th, diminished 7th, Neapolitan 6th • Dissonances: false relation, suspension, appoggiatura
Texture	• Monophonic (one solo line) • Homophonic (chordal, melody and chords) • Arpeggios (broken chords), Alberti Bass • Polyphonic (2 or more independent lines) • Fugal • Detached (staccato) or sustained (legato) chords • Parts in unison or octaves • The number of parts in the music (2, 3, 4, etc.) • Parallel motion, e.g., 3rds/6ths • Contrary motion • Pedals (tonic/dominant, in the bass/inverted) • Imitation • Canon (exact imitation) • Antiphony (Call and Response in some cultures) • Ostinato (Riff in popular music/jazz)
Forces	The voices/instruments/sounds used in the music: • Tessitura (register or range) • Glissando, falls, pitch bends • Strings: bowed, plucked, harmonics, muted • Piano: sustain/soft pedals • Guitars: acoustic/electric, rhythm/lead, clean/distorted
Context	The purpose or occasion for which the music was created: • Religious ceremony or ritual • Public entertainment, e.g., concert, theatre • Mass media, e.g., studio recording, film and television • Dancing or celebration • Private entertainment, e.g., for a patron (royalty, aristocracy), for family/friends to perform themselves

Section A

PRESCRIBED WORKS 2016

PETITE MESSE SOLENNELLE (1863) – GIOACHINO ROSSINI

The Mass

Mass (also known as Holy Communion or Eucharist) is one of the most important acts of worship in the Christian religion. The main purpose of the worship or service is to re-enact the Last Supper, which Jesus asked his disciples to do in his memory. As early as the 7th century it became customary for the fixed parts of the Catholic Mass text to be set to music. The fixed parts of the text are called *Kyrie, Gloria, Credo, Sanctus, Benedictus* and *Agnus Dei*. To these sections Rossini added the *O Salutaris*, a verse from a hymn, and the *Preludio religioso*, an instrumental piece for piano or harmonium.

Rossini's Mass

When studying this work it must be remembered that Rossini (1792–1868) wrote most of his operas in the first part of the 19th century, which marks the changeover from the Classical style to the Romantic. It should also be borne in mind that he 'retired' from composing opera after completing *William Tell* in 1829 at the age of 38, and at the height of considerable fame and fortune. Thirty-four years later, when Rossini composed *Petite messe solennelle*, Romantic music was evolving ever more rapidly towards the eventual breakdown of tonality, but at the same time there was also a greater awareness of the European music of the past. Thus it follows that you will find elements of many styles, past and present, in this work, especially the *opera buffa* (comic opera) for which Rossini is best remembered, as he acknowledged in his own dedication to God on the autograph score:

> Good God – behold completed this poor little Mass – is it indeed sacred music [*la musique sacrée*] that I have just written, or merely some damned music [*la sacré musique*]? You know well, I was born for comic opera. Little science, a little heart, that is all. So may you be blessed, and grant me Paradise!

Even the title is tongue in cheek: this Mass is not little (it lasts well over an hour), and it is not necessarily solemn! But it certainly showcases Rossini's natural ability to compose free-flowing music and his gift for beautiful songlike melodies, the musical element he prized above all others.

The most useful way to analyse this piece for examination purposes is to look at the use of the musical elements in the light of the many styles and influences in each of the 14 movements. The *Petite messe solennelle* is organized into two parts, each containing seven movements. Remember that movements 2–7 together make up the *Gloria* and 8–10 make up the *Credo*. Locations are based on the Novello Vocal Score last reprinted in 1997.

Instrumentation

Rossini's original score calls for Soprano, Alto, Tenor and Bass soloists, an SATB chorus and an accompaniment of 2 pianos and a harmonium. The first piano part takes the majority share of the accompanying, with the second piano and harmonium either doubling the first piano or the singers. The harmonium is a type of reed organ and belongs to the keyboard family of instruments: like a pipe organ it requires an air supply, which is powered by the performer via two foot-operated bellows.

1. Kyrie – Christe

Background	Traditionally the first part of a Mass setting, the words *Kyrie eleison* and *Christe eleison* ('Lord have mercy, Christ have mercy') are derived from Greek as well as Latin. At the start of the Mass rite those present ask God for forgiveness so that they may take part in the service with a pure heart. Rossini's choral writing here is full of sincerity but the quirky syncopations of the piano part and the occasional dramatic outburst reveal his *opera buffa* roots.	
Structure and Tonality	The layout of the words steer most composers towards a Ternary form structure, and Rossini was no exception. Like many Romantic composers, Rossini used tonality to define and reinforce his musical structures. A – *Kyrie* 35 bars, starting in A minor, comprising an 8-bar introduction, which is repeated with choral entries, a short link that modulates to the relative (C) major. This is followed by 2 x 4-bar Classical style question-and-answer phrases, the	

	second of which starts in C minor but ends back in C major. This section is rounded off with an 8-bar phrase featuring dotted rhythms, and some octaves in the final bars to match those at the start. B – *Christe* 22 bars, in C minor, an **a cappella** setting for the SATB chorus. A¹ – *Kyrie* 33 bars, following on from the B section in C minor but ending in the tonic (A) major instead of the minor. The introduction is shorter and all the earlier phrases are present, but Rossini adds a new more-chromatic phrase (b75) before the final phrase with the dotted rhythms (b81). As before, the whole of A¹ is framed by piano and harmonium octaves.	
Melody	A – There are 3 main themes: • The 1-bar figure in the piano left hand (LH); mostly stepwise with a falling octave at the end of the bar. This is repeated and then used in a rising sequence before chromatically falling back to where it started.	b2–8
	• A Classical **question-and-answer** phrase in the Soprano: Question – descending C major arpeggio figure decorated with an appoggiatura and an anticipation (b19³⁻⁴), then an upward minor 7th leap followed by a syncopated stepwise descent back to G on an imperfect cadence.	b18³–22²
	Answer – similar melody to the question, but starting with a C minor arpeggio and modified to pass through E♭ major, finishing on a perfect cadence back in C major.	b22³–26
	• A shorter question-and-answer phrase based on dotted rhythms.	b26–30
	B – Features Renaissance-style stepwise movement, with occasional leaps. Notice the rising scale in the Bass (b37) is inverted in the Tenor 2 bars later.	b36
	A¹ – As before, but with a new chromatic melody in A minor, with a striking diminished 5th (b77⁴ Soprano).	b75–81

Harmony	Rossini's tonal structure is decorated with a series of rich chromatic chords featuring: • Diminished 7ths (b7³ F#–C–D#–A). • Augmented 6ths (b7⁴ F–A–C–D#) – see below. Other chromatic chords include: • Secondary dominants (b11⁴ B major is V of V in A minor). • Extended chords (b27¹ V⁹ D–F#–A–C–E and b27³ G¹³ G–B–D–F–E).	
	Switching from the major to the minor of the same key was a common tonal shift in the Romantic period, e.g., the sudden changes between C major and minor in the first *Kyrie*.	b17–26
Texture and Instrumentation	A – After the opening octaves, the piano plays detached syncopated chords over LH octaves, while the harmonium doubles the piano with contrasting sustained chords. The initial choral entries are imitative, but from b12 onwards the choir textures are mostly homophonic. The harmonium doubles the choral parts.	b1–8
	B – A polyphonic setting in the style of 16th-century Renaissance sacred music. Much of the imitation can be more accurately described as a double **canon** between Basses and Altos, and Tenors and Sopranos.	b36
Rhythm	Section A: • Syncopated RH piano chords, together with the LH octaves create a jerky but continuous semiquaver pattern throughout this section. • Syncopation in the Soprano against the regular crotchets of the rest of the choir. • Dramatic double dotted rhythms. • Occasional fanfare-like dotted rhythms in the harmonium between choral phrases.	 b20–21 b26–27 b20
	Section B: Change of time signature to 4/2 (4 minims in a bar), resulting in longer note values, including the **breve** (b39 Bass), which equals 8 crotchets. This is also a nod to the Renaissance, given that much music from that time was notated using similar rhythmic values.	

2. *Gloria – Laudamus*

Background	The *Gloria* is a hymn of praise to God. There are a large number of words to set to music for the *Gloria*, and from the Baroque period onwards it became customary to spread the text across several movements, which could nonetheless be taken as a musical whole. In Rossini's setting there are 6 movements (numbers 2–7), the first and last of which act as a framework by sharing the same opening music and using the chorus. By contrast the middle movements are given to the soloists in various combinations. The influence of opera can clearly be seen in movements 4–6 which, instead of ending on a clear final cadence, segue into the following movement.	
Structure	82 bars, 2 very contrasting sections in Binary form: • A – Allegro maestoso (fast and majestic). • Short link passage for piano. • B – A longer, slightly slower section mostly for the soloists; the chorus join in towards the end.	b1–18 b19–24 b25–end
Melody	There are several examples of word painting here: • *Gloria in excelsis Deo* (*Glory to God in the Highest*) has a rising fanfare-like arpeggio figure. • *Et in terra pax* (*And on the Earth Peace*) the Bass soloist sings a wide-ranging (spanning a major 13th) melody that softly descends down to a low F. • *Glorificamus te* (*We glorify you*) features an elaborate, mostly stepwise phrase, rising and falling with melismas.	b5–7 b26–33 b61–65 (Alto)
Harmony and Tonality	A – Begins in the tonic key of F major and modulates to the dominant at b16, with the link passage returning to the tonic. Mostly diatonic harmony. B – Starts and ends in F major, with some mediant modulations along the way (b37 A♭ major, b49 C♭ major, b59 E minor) before returning to the dominant (b61) and tonic (b65). • The various keys of Section B are reinforced by perfect cadences and a I–IV ostinato chord progression. • Major chords are regularly substituted by minor chords (e.g., F major for F minor). • Enharmonic change; C♭ major and F♭m triads become B major and Em respectively. • Plagal cadence at the end.	 b33–36 b58–59

Texture and Instrumentation	Section A – the texture changes frequently to achieve some striking effects:	
	• A series of detached **ff** spread piano chords reinforced by sustained harmonium chords, followed by dramatic silences.	b1–8
	• Monophonic Soprano entry, answered homophonically by all voices unaccompanied.	b9–14
	• This is followed by a tutti homophonic climax on *Gloria*, decorated by piano arpeggios.	b15–18
	Link: simple **ppp** piano octaves	
	Section B:	
	• Melody and ostinato chords.	b26–33
	• Antiphony between soloists (e.g., Soprano, answered by Alto, Tenor, Bass).	b37–45
	• Close imitation between the soloists (*Glorificamus*).	b61–69
	• Chorus rejoin soloists at b69. All singers sing **sotto voce** on the last phrase.	
Rhythm	Section A:	
	• Flamboyant demisemiquaver flourishes in the piano.	b1–3
	• Fanfare-like double dotted rhythms announce the choral entries.	b9 & 12
	Section B:	
	• Double dotted rhythms are softened into triplets (e.g., Soprano *Benedicimus te*).	b41–42
	• Irregular phrase lengths in the piano ostinato chords cut across the 2/4 metre (e.g., 6 beats, 7 beats, 7 beats).	b25–34

3. Gratias

Background	A lyrical setting of the words 'We give thanks to you for your great glory', for Alto, Tenor and Bass soli and piano.	
Structure and Tonality	114 bars, in **ternary form** with some features for piano only, which were borrowed from the German **lieder** genre perfected by Schubert and others in the early 19th century:	
	• Prelude/Introduction (A major).	b0–23
	• A – A **fugato** with entries for Bass (A major, b24), Alto (E major, b33) and Tenor (C major, b42) soli.	b24–50
	• B – A more agitated section based on the dominant of A major, with a **ff** climax at b56. This is followed by a highly chromatic piano Interlude.	b51–66

	• A¹ – A reworking of the main fugato subject, followed by a new theme at b76, repeated unchanged from b84 (A major).	b67–92
	• Coda and a piano Postlude, using ideas from the opening Prelude (b92–95 = b16–19).	b92–114

Melody	Section A:
	• The fugato subject is based on a simple crotchet-quaver-quaver motif, which mostly descends over a narrow range. It is decorated with acciaccaturas and a turn at the cadence. The phrasing is *asymmetric*; 4 bars b24–27, 5 ¼ bars b28–33¹.
	• There are 2 simple countersubjects:
	  - The 3 offbeat quavers, which shadow the piano chords (Bass b33, Alto b42)
	  - The auxiliary note figure (Bass b42²)	

	Section B: • A powerful descending minor 7th leap for the Tenor and Bass, word-painting on *magnam* (great).	b51–55
	Section A¹: • New theme at b76 is an inversion of the minor 7th leap first heard in B, followed by a descending semiquaver scale.	
	Coda: • **Augmentation** of the Prelude ending b20–23 at the end of the Postlude.	b106–114
Harmony and Tonality	Tonality is mostly centred on A major, with modulation to the dominant b33, and a median modulation to C major b42. Despite the clear tonal structure, the harmony is at times both complex and diverse.	
	Prelude: • The tonic key is initially blurred by the opening French augmented 6th chord (F–A–B–D#), but is quickly followed by V⁷ of A major.	b1–4
	• Brief visit to C# minor.	b10–11
	• Tonic pedal underpinning a series of chromatic chords including diminished 7th and V¹³ (both b19).	b16–20¹
	• Neapolitan 6th in 2nd inversion (F–D–F–B♭).	b20²
	• Triple suspension on the final cadence.	b22
	Section A: • Most triads are enriched with added 7ths (e.g., b24² Bm⁷, E⁷ piano RH).	
	Section B: • Dominant pedal on E.	b51–59
	• Chromatic descending sequence based on alternating diminished 7ths and major chords.	b60–63¹

	Section A¹: • The new theme at b76–92¹ is entirely **diatonic**. • Harmony. • Simple alternation of I and V⁷. • Descending sequence, with 4–3 suspensions in the Tenor.	b76–79 b80²–84¹
Texture and Instrument-ation	Prelude: • Chordal texture. • Use of silent bars for dramatic effect. • RH chords over LH octaves, repeated an octave higher. • Melody-dominated homophony over a tonic pedal. Section A: • Fugato in 3 solo voices, with piano RH chords and LH octaves. Section B: • Imitation between Bass and Tenor. • Octaves for all parts at the *ff* climax. Section A¹: • Fugato subject reworked with homophonic voices and flowing RH piano semiquaver arpeggios. • New theme imitated in the 3 voices. Coda: • Sustained sotto voce chords in voices.	b1–4 b7 b8–14 b16–23 b24–50 b51–55 b56–58 b67–75 b76–79 b98–104
Rhythm	• Operatic fanfare-like rhythms at the start. • Quaver pulse results in dotted rhythms being notated as dotted quaver-demisemiquaver. • Some phrases have a syncopated start.	b0–5 b17 b16, b51

4. *Domine Deus*

Background	A lively, march-style 'aria' for Tenor solo and piano accompaniment.	
Structure	164 bars, in **ternary form** with some features for piano only, which were borrowed from the German **lieder** genre perfected by Schubert and others in the early 19th century: • Prelude/Introduction (D major), following on from the A major dominant preparation at the end of the previous *Gratias*.	 b1–16

	• A – 44 bars, regular phrases (mostly 4 bars) in D major with modulations to the tonic minor (D minor, b26) and the relative minor (B minor, b42). This is followed by a piano Interlude derived from the Prelude, which ends in B minor.	b17–60
	• B – A more subdued section in the relative minor, word-painting *Agnus Dei* (*Lamb of God*), modulating to its dominant (F♯ minor, b68) and returning towards D major (V⁷c, b87).	b61–87
	• A – Repeated as before, without the Interlude.	b88–123
	• Coda and a piano Postlude, using ideas from the opening Prelude (e.g., piano RH: b123–124 = b8–9).	b123–164
Melody	This movement highlights Rossini's skill as a melody writer. The piano and the Tenor have their own melodic material, although both have a dotted rhythm on the 4th beat in common. Prelude: • 2 main motifs:	
	• The opening auxiliary note figure F♯– F♯–G–F♯ (piano RH) is repeated as a rising sequence.	b1–7
	• The 3-note rhythmic motif B–A–A, repeated with wide disjunct leaps.	b8²–12¹
	Section A: • Most of the Tenor melody here is created from 2 motifs:	
	• The upward major 6th leap (*x*).	b18¹⁻³
	• Another auxiliary note figure E–F♯–E similar to that in the piano prelude (*y*).	b18⁴–19¹
	• Interval *x* is changed to, e.g., a minor 7th (b20) and a minor 6th (b26).	
	• Auxiliary note *y* is inverted (b35 G–F♯–G).	
	• *x* and *y* are used in a descending sequence.	b38–45
	• The rise up to the climax is decorated with appoggiaturas (e.g., A♯ b47) and an accented passing note (D b50³). The climax itself (top A b51) is itself a suspension resolving to G.	

	Section B:
	 • Melodically simpler than A; generally, the piano RH uses *x* as a call, answered by the Tenor (e.g., b62²–68).
	
	 Coda:
	 • Some further motivic developments; the first note of leap *x* has been omitted, and auxiliary note *y* is inverted.
	 • A striking series of accented ornaments can be seen in the Tenor b133:
	   - beat 1, F# suspension
	   - beat 2, A# chromatic appoggiatura
	   - beat 3, C# auxiliary note
	   - beat 4, F# appoggiatura
	 • Auxiliary note *y* is both inverted and augmented to crotchets at the final Tenor climax.
		
		 b124–127
		
		 b133
		
		 b147 & 149

Harmony and Tonality	• Tonality is clearly linked to the ternary structure. It is mostly centred on D major in both Section A's, and the relative minor in Section B.
	 • There are visits to more distant keys in some places:
	   • D minor (tonic minor – a common 19th-century key change)
	   • F# major (b76), D# minor (b80)
	   • E♭ major – a brief Neapolitan-like key change in the Coda popular in the Baroque period, which quickly resolves back to the tonic
	
	 Prelude:
	 • Almost entirely diatonic.
	
	 Section A:
	 • A clever chromatic chord progression is used to return to the tonic:
	
	   - b34, diminished 7th on E, G minor 2nd inversion
	   - b35, augmented 6th on E♭ 3rd inversion, C⁷
		
		 b26–29
		
		 b131 & 143
		
		 b34–37

	- b36, Em 2nd inversion, French augmented 6th on B♭ - b37, A^7 (V^7 of D) • Successive dominant pedals in D major and B minor. Coda: • Mediant modulation to F♯ major. • Tonic pedal in the piano postlude. • Ends on an imperfect cadence in F major (Ic b159, V^7 b160) to link into the following 'Qui tollis'.	b38–45 b149 b151–155
Texture and Instrumentation	• Melody-dominated homophony for the most part; much of the Tenor melody is accompanied by detached piano bass and chords. • Many Tenor phrase ends are regularly filled by short, imitative piano RH melodies using auxiliary motif y. • In the reprise of A, these imitative melodies switch to the LH. • The piano solo sections often have the RH melody played in octaves. • Tenor part occasionally doubled by piano RH. • Running quaver triplet arpeggio piano accompaniment in the Coda.	 b18–19 b89 b1–8 b38–53 b123 onwards
Rhythm	• March style emphasized by a strict Allegro 4/4, dotted rhythms, fanfare-like triplets (b37, piano) and detached piano chords almost throughout. • Two important rhythmic motifs at the start (piano RH): - The quaver-quaver rest-minim accents the 2nd beat of much of the melodic material. - The dotted quaver-semiquaver-quaver motif is developed in all of the piano solo sections. • Syncopation in the Tenor part. • Running quaver triplet piano accompaniment in the Coda.	 b1$^{1-3}$ b1^4–2^1 b23–24 b123 onwards

5. *Qui Tollis*

Background	A more subdued movement asking for mercy to be granted and prayers to be heard. The music reflects this in several ways (e.g., minor key, slower tempo) and is scored for Soprano and Alto soli, piano and harmonium, which adds to the reflective atmosphere.	
Structure	112 bars in **ternary form**, with an introduction and a coda, which also act as linking passages to the movements before and after.	
	• Introduction/Prelude: a continuation of the dominant preparation for the tonic key F minor.	b1–7
	• A – F minor, with regular 4-bar phrases.	b8–35
	• 1-bar link, dominant preparation (V of D♭ major).	b36
	• B – D♭ major, modulating to A♭ major b45 and C major b53, setting up a dominant pedal for F minor?	b37–57
	• A¹ – Rossini has other ideas; he slides into the distant key of E major! F minor returns 4 bars later, along with the original music from A. The original first phrase is not forgotten; instead it reappears later at b81 but now in F major.	b58–89
	• Coda – mostly in F major, 3 x 8 bar phrases. The second phrase is a variant of the first; the last is based on the Introduction/Prelude, ending on octave A's to segue into the next movement.	b89–112
Melody	Section A: Soprano part • The whole melody has regular 4 bar phrases. • Most of the phrases fall, as though asking for forgiveness. • Auxiliary notes are frequently used. • Range is only 1 octave (F–F), which is seen most clearly in the final phrase.	b11⁴–15 b13², 15² b32–35
	Section B: Soprano part • Expressive 8-bar question-and-answer phrase; the 1st phrase features rising, sweeping arpeggios. The 2nd falls back via a chromatic passing note (F♭) and disjunct 5ths and 6ths. Decorated with turns b38 and 44. Repeated by the Alto a 4th lower. • Rising chromatic sequence	b37⁴–45 b53–57

	Section A¹:	
	• Some variants of the opening phrase:	
	- Rising instead of falling	b57⁴–61
	- Minims of b14 replaced with a more elaborate rhythm and appoggiaturas	b84
	• Auxiliary notes from A repeated and extended.	b91–93
	Coda:	
	• Final vocal phrase decorated with a grace note and trill.	b108³
Harmony and Tonality	• **Mediant modulation** from F minor to D♭ major.	b35–37
	• Tonic pedal, piano LH.	b8–15
	• Tonal harmony decorated with wide variety of chromatic piano chords:	
	- **Augmented 6th** 3rd inversion (B–F–A♭–D♭)	b16³
	- **Neapolitan 6th** (B♭–D♭–G♭), followed by V⁷d and Ib (F minor)	b20³–21
	- Augmented triad (D♭–F–A)	b39
	• Chain of expressive 7–6 suspensions in the Alto.	b32–33
	• Slide into E major achieved via diminished 7th on C, augmented 6th on C, Ic in E major.	b57–58
Texture and Instrumentation	Section A:	
	• Parallel 3rds between Soprano and Alto accompanied by flowing piano arpeggios.	b12–19
	• Harmonium plays contrasting sustained chords, which shadow the soli and piano.	b16–23
	Section B:	
	• Melody-dominated homophony.	b37–51
	• Piano texture changes to a mixture of arpeggios and detached chords.	b37
	Coda:	
	• Imitation between Soprano and Alto.	b89²–91²
	• Soprano and Alto doubling the piano part.	b105–108
Rhythm	• Syncopation, piano RH.	b1
	• Unbroken semiquaver accompaniment throughout most of the movement.	
	• Speech rhythm in the opening vocal phrases, e.g.,	b11⁴–12³
	• *Qui* | *Tol -- lis.*	
	• Double-dotted rhythms.	b53–57
	• **Polyrhythm** between triplets (soli and harmonium) and semiquavers (piano).	b84, 88
	• *a piacere* ('at pleasure'); the singers can sing the rhythms freely at this instruction. Used at the end of an aria/duet since the Baroque period.	b108

6. Quoniam

Background	A substantial **aria**-like movement for Bass solo and piano in the style of Schubert.	
Structure and Melody	Best described as a loose **strophic** structure with 3 verses, which uses 5 different themes arranged in different combinations:	
	Introduction/Prelude – after a brief adagio link from the *Qui tollis*, the 3 main themes are presented:	
	1. Rising and falling octave leaps split between the hands.	b4–12
	2. A syncopated idea starting on the 4th beat of the bar, suspended over the bar line and tied to a short, dotted triadic motif.	$b14^4$–22^1
	3. Another syncopated idea starting on the 2nd beat of the bar using auxiliary notes; this idea is only heard in the piano.	$b22^2$–28
	Verse 1: a 4th theme for the Bass, which is heard only once; it uses a falling arpeggio b29–31, wide leaps b37–38, and regular sequential phrasing b29–41. Followed by an extended version of the 2nd idea and the piano Interlude (3rd idea).	b29–66
	Verse 2: longer than verse 1. The 1st theme is followed by a new 5th theme b78, using rising and falling 4ths b83–5, and a rising chromatic sequence up to a top E climax b97. Followed by another variant of the 2nd theme and another Interlude.	b66–127
	Verse 3: similar to verse 2. The 1st, 5th and 2nd themes are all repeated a semitone higher. The Interlude is replaced by a Coda.	b127–182
	Coda: based on the 2nd idea.	b182–189
	Postlude: for piano, based on the 3rd theme repeated in a rising sequence until the dominant of F major is established ready for the next movement.	b189–209

Melody	<ul><li>For notes on the main themes, see Structure.</li><li>Frequent use of ornaments in the Bass solo:
	  - Turn
	  - Chromatic appoggiatura (B♯)
	  - Chromatic passing note (F double sharp)
	  - Trill and auxiliary note decorating the cadence</li><li>Wide melodic range of a minor 13th for Bass solo (low A to high F).</li></ul>
		
		b32
		b51
		b54²
		b59

Harmony and Tonality	<ul><li>Largely centred on A major, but modulates to a wide range of keys, all confirmed with perfect cadences, e.g., C♯ minor b66, C major b98, F major b139, D♭ major b159.</li><li>Ends on V of F major to segue into *Cum Sancto Spiritu*.</li><li>Frequently uses harmonic sequences to modulate to other keys, e.g., b89–94, based on 2-bar progression V⁷d–Ib of D major, then E♭ major, E minor.</li><li>Typically, operatic V¹³ formed from piano G⁷ chord with Bass high E on top.</li><li>Chromatic piano chords:
	  - Dominant minor 9th E–G♯–D–F
	  - French augmented 6th F–A–B–D♯
	  - German augmented 6th F–A–C–D♯</li><li>Suspensions, e.g., 4–3 A–G♯, 2nd theme</li></ul>
		
		b97³
		
		b148³
		b13³
		b21²
		b19

Texture and Instrumenta-tion	<ul><li>Bass solo and piano have an equal partnership, similar to the German Lieder of Schubert; both have their own themes and the long trills (b13 piano, b59 Bass).</li><li>Switching between piano RH and LH of the melody and detached chordal accompaniment.</li><li>Broken octaves, piano RH.</li><li>Melody-dominated homophony.</li><li>Bass melody doubled in the piano RH an octave higher (also doubled in the LH b99–102)</li><li>Melody over sustained chords</li></ul>	 b4–14 b20–21 b29–43 b48–55 b78–97

Rhythm	• Common time throughout, Adagio b1–3, Allegro moderato for the remainder	
	• Once again, dotted rhythms play an important part in both melody and accompaniment	
	• Running quaver chords, often switched between the hands of the piano	b4–14
	• Syncopation, piano LH	b37–40
	• Syncopated RH piano chords	b78–97

7. Cum Sancto Spiritu

Background	An uplifting **fugue** in F major for the chorus to round off the *Gloria*, and a glorious way to end Part 1 (Act 1?) of this Mass. Rossini brings all his contrapuntal and dramatic skills to bear on this movement.	
Structure	• Introduction, F major – a reprise of the introduction from the 2nd movement, which unifies the *Gloria* as a whole.	b1–25
	• Fugal **exposition**, F major:	b26–54
	- **subject** (Soprano)	b26–33
	- **counter-subject** 1 (Alto)	b27–32
	- tonal **answer** (Alto)	b33–40
	- **counter-subject** 2 (Soprano)	b40–43
	• **Episode** – modulates from F to B♭ major via	b54–83
	• other keys (e.g., G minor b58, D minor b66).	
	• Middle entries, B♭ major.	b84–112
	• Episode – longer than before, modulates from B♭ back to F major via some very distant keys (A♭ major b137, G♭ major b150–152).	b112–161
	• Final entries, F major in **stretto.**	b162–178
	• At this point Rossini departs from the traditional fugue structure, with another episode.	b178–206
	• Reprise of the *Gloria* introduction.	b206–225
	• Coda on *Amen.*	b225–268
Melody	• Fugue subject (Soprano): 8 bars, opens with a decisive upward minor 7th leap, which briefly implies subdominant key of B♭ major. F major returns with a rising tonic arpeggio up to top F climax, before modulating to the dominant C major.	b26–33
	• Counter-subject 1 (Alto) has 2 motifs; a simple F–E–F idea mostly in minims b27–29, and a disjunct syncopated idea b30.	b27–32

	• Counter-subject 2 (Soprano): a conjunct 3-note figure used in a rising sequence. Rossini freely interchanges ideas from both counter-subjects in the part writing.	b40–47

	• Episode themes are derived and extended from fragments first heard in the exposition:
	  1. Minor 7th leap Tenor b54 = Soprano b26
	  2. F–G–F–G motif b54^2 = Soprano b45^1
	  3. D–E♭–C–D soprano b56 = Alto b46^2
		b54–57

	• Two climaxes in the coda; Soprano top G b234, then top A b254.	
Harmony and Tonality	• The subject entries are centred on F major, whereas the episodes visit a wider range of keys, e.g., G♭ major.	
	• Dominant pedals are used to move from episodes into subject entries, e.g., F pedal leading to Middle entries in B♭.	b76–84
	• Some dissonant chromatic harmony in the episodes, e.g., variety of major, minor and diminished triads clashing with a C pedal.	b145–48
	• Striking Augmented 6th chord on D♭, 3rd inversion (B–D♭–F–A♭) approaching the final choir perfect cadence in F major.	b256
Texture and Instrument-ation	• Mostly fugal texture in the choral parts.	
	• Harmonium paraphrases the choir and piano throughout.	
	• Contrasting detached and sustained chords from the piano and harmonium throughout most of the movement.	
	• Contrary motion between all the parts at the start of the episodes.	b54–62
	• Chain of imitative suspensions between Bass and Soprano.	b62–70
	• Dominant pedal in Bass and piano LH.	b76–83
	• **Stretto** in the final entries.	b162–166
	• Coda becomes increasingly homophonic.	b225^2
	• Widely spaced piano chords in tremolo quavers.	b246–253
Rhythm, Dynamics and Tempo	Excitement in the movement is created and sustained by several features:	
	• A very wide range of dynamic markings, from ***pppp*** (b135) to ***fff*** (b254) in the piano and harmonium.	
	• Allegro maestoso (fast and majestic) 4/4 time, accelerating by changing to 2/2 time (b26) and 'Animando un poco' (a little more animated).	
	• Demisemiquaver flourishes.	b1–7
	• Piano accompaniment features running quavers in the LH and syncopated RH chords throughout most of the movement.	
	• Rapid tremolo quavers in the piano.	b246–253

8. Credo

Background	Credo means 'I believe', and the text sets out the main tenets of the Christian faith. As with the Gloria, there is a large amount of text to be set to music, so composers tended to spread the Credo across several musical numbers. Here, Rossini composed three movements; two for soli and chorus (Credo and Et Resurrexit), with an aria for Soprano solo in between (Crucifixus). The first movement tempo is unusually marked Allegro Cristiano – 'fast, in a Christian manner'.	

Structure	The Credo melody is used throughout as a unifying motto theme.
	Section A:
	• Consisting of 3 principal themes:
	  - The Credo motto
	  - a **pp** figure mostly in minims
	  - a lyrical theme passed around the soli
	Section B:
	• New 4th theme; an imitative choral passage that modulates through E♭ F and G minor climaxing with the word painting on Descendit de coelis.
	Section A^1:
	• A brief reprise of the motto theme and the **pp** figure.
	• Coda, which modulates to V of A♭ major, to segue into the Crucifixus.
		b3–10
		
		b1–83
		
		b9–10^1
		b10^3–18^1
		b22^4–24^3
		b84–104
		
		b105–120
		
		b120–136

Melody	• The Credo motto theme has a distinctive semibreve-crotchet rhythm. • The **pp** minim figure starts on one note, representing belief in one God (in unum Deum). • The lyrical 2-bar theme for the soli has a narrow range initially, but this is followed by a downwards octave leap. • Word setting almost entirely syllabic. • Word-painting on Descendit de coelis (He came down from heaven); **ff** climax as the Soprano and the piano descend down through their range.	b3–4 b10–12 b22^4–24^3 b96–104
Harmony and Tonality	• Tonic key of E major not fully established until the perfect cadence at b17–18. The tonality is disrupted immediately by a half- diminished 7th on F♯ (F♯–A–C♮–E), then by a mediant modulation to C major b14.	b1–18

	• Tonic pedal on E underneath the chromatic progression I–I⁺ (augmented)–IVc–V⁷–I.	b18–22
	• Diatonic 2-bar sequence including Renaissance-style 4–3 suspensions.	b23–28
	• A number of rich chromatic chords:	
	- V 11th of C with 3rd omitted (G–D–F– A–C)	b13
	- V 13th of E (B–D♯–A–G♯)	b17
	- French Augmented 6th on D♭ (D♭–F–G–B)	b87⁴
	• Modulation to distant keys, e.g., E♭, F and G minor before returning to E major on *Descendit de coelis*.	b84–96
Texture and Instrumentation	Section A:	
	• A variety of textures can be seen in the opening bars:	
	- Piano broken chords	b1
	- Harmonium sustained chords combined with piano tremolo chords	b3
	- Homorhythmic choir and harmonium	b9
	• Homophonic choral chords.	b14–22
	• Imitative entries for the soli.	b22–27
	Section B:	
	• Piano in octaves, with imitative entries for the chorus.	b84–96
	• *Descendit*: Homorhythmic SATB, accompanied by piano octaves and harmonium detached chords.	b96–101
Rhythm	• Opening fanfare-like rhythm always heard before the *Credo* motto theme, and also used in the piano accompaniment in quieter passages, e.g., b18–31.	
	• Semiquaver tremolo piano chords.	b3
	• Dramatic double-dotted rhythms on *Descendit de coelis*.	b97–101
	• Fragmented dotted rhythms in the closing piano link to *Crucifixus*.	b128–135

9. Crucifixus

Background	The words here describe Christ's crucifixion and have inspired many composers over time. Rossini's setting for Soprano solo is heartfelt and expressive, if perhaps a little melodramatic.	
Structure	A strophic, song-like structure:	
	• Section A.	b1–21
	• Section A¹: the opening *Crucifixus* motif is modified and extended.	b21–51

Melody	• *Crucifixus* motif is mostly stepwise and descends to depict sadness.	b2–3
	• *Crucifixus* motif is later developed as a rising sequence.	b22–29
	• The sadness of the words is shown melodically in other ways:	
	- Frequent appoggiaturas	$b3^1, 5^1$
	- Falling diminished 4th (D♭–A♮) on *Pontio*	b10
	- Falling chromatic passing note (D)	$b13^2$
	• Dramatic word painting on *passus et sepultus est* (He died and was buried); starts with a climax on a high G appoggiatura, descends through a major 9th, chromatic passing note (F♭), before settling on a low E♭ on 'buried'.	b19–20
Harmony and Tonality	• Tonic key of A♭ major: mediant relationship with the E major of the movements before and after.	
	• Very chromatic harmony throughout, resulting in frequent modulations, e.g., C♭ major b17.	
	• Rising sequence on *Crucifixus* motif uses mediant modulations; B major, D major, F major, returning to A♭ major.	b22–29
	• A number of rich chromatic chords:	
	- Diminished 7th on A♮	$b1^3$
	- German Augmented 6th on F♭	$b6^3$
	- French Augmented 6th on D♭	$b8^3$
	• Enharmonic writing; F♭⁷–B♭♭ = E⁷–A major.	$b45^3–46^2$
	• Circle of dominant 7ths.	$b47^3–48^3$
Texture and Instrument-ation	• Melody-dominated homophony throughout.	
	• Accompaniment combines detached piano chords with sustained harmonium chords.	
Rhythm	• Fairly slow, 4/4.	
	• Lilting, syncopated piano chords throughout.	
	• *Crucifixus* motif starts on the weaker 2nd beat of the bar.	b2
	• Double-dotted rhythms on *etiam pro nobis*.	b6
	• Quavers on *passus* emphasised with accents.	b19

10. Et Resurrexit

Background	The last of the 3 movements that make up the *Credo*. Rossini reprises much of the music heard in the first movement, and finishes with an exciting choral fugue in a similar fashion to the *Cum Sancto Spiritu* movement of the Gloria.	

Structure	384 bars, with a central fugue section. This chorus is best thought of as being through-composed. The *Credo* motto theme is again used to unify the structure.	
	Introduction: (b1–28)	
	• Follows straight on from the preceding *Crucifixus*. Rossini cleverly uses an enharmonic change to modulate immediately to V of E major. The striking ***ff*** opening tells of Christ being raised from the dead on the third day. Ends with a reminder of the motto theme.	
	Section A: (b29–154)	
	• Rossini alternates the principal themes heard before in the *Credo*:	
	- the lyrical theme passed around the soli	b34–35
	- a 5th new theme treated sequentially	b44⁴–48
	- the imitative choral passage	b58²–70
	- the ***pp*** figure mostly in minims	b72–82
	- The *Credo* motto	b109
	Section B: Fugue (b155–284)	
	• Fugal **exposition**, E major:	b155–184
	- **subject** (Soprano)	b155–162
	- **counter-subject** 1 (Tenor) introduced immediately instead of with the answer	b156–162
	- tonal **answer** (Alto)	b162–169
	- **counter-subject** 1 (Bass)	b163–169
	- **counter-subject** 2 (Soprano)	b162–169
	- **subject** (Tenor)	b169
	- tonal **answer** (Bass)	b176
	• **Episode** – modulates from E to A major via other keys (e.g., F♯ major b188, C♯ minor b195).	b184–204
	• Middle entries, A major.	b204–232
	• Episode – longer than before, modulates from A back to E major. Long dominant pedal B, b252.	b232–267
	• Final entries, E major in **stretto**.	b267–284
	• Coda on *Amen* (b284–384).	
	• 1st passage initially based on the Episode theme, becomes homophonic.	b284–314
	• 1st passage repeated without change.	b314–344
	• Music modulates to G♯ major and stops on an ***fff*** chord. Followed by a brief soli reminder of *In unum deum* from the earlier movement, and a final, decisive *Credo* from the chorus as a perfect cadence in the tonic E major.	b344–384

Melody	Introduction:	
	• Word-painting with the Soprano rising octave leap on *resurrexit*; answered by rapid rising piano scales, e.g., b22.	b2–3
	Section A:	
	• For a description of the earlier *Credo* themes, refer to the notes for movement 8.	
	• Additional 5th theme has a narrow range of a 5th, and gradually rises via a succession of auxiliary notes. Treated sequentially in subsequent repeats.	b44⁴–48
	• Word-painting on 'resurrection (*ff*) of the dead (*pp*)'.	b138–143
	Section B:	
	• Fugue subject – after an opening tonic arpeggio, the subject descends chromatically down the E major scale.	b155–162
	• Counter-subject 1 – by contrast ascends the E major scale mostly in minims at the same time as the subject. Normally the counter-subject is not heard until the entry of the answer.	b156–162
	• Counter-subject 2 – more fragmented and syncopated, with a range of 1 octave.	b162–169
	• Episode – a rising figure mostly in steps and perfect 4ths.	
Harmony and Tonality	• Enharmonic change moves quickly from the *Crucifixus* key of A♭ major to V of E major. Notice how the Soprano E♭ becomes a D♯. E major finally established at b29.	b1–3
	• The new theme is used to modulate through a circle of 5ths; G♯ major b44, C♯ b48, F♯ b53, B major b58.	b44–58
	• A number of rich chromatic chords:	
	- V 11th of G with 3rd omitted (D–C–E–G), moving to V⁷	b77¹
	- French Augmented 6th on D (D–F♯–G♯–B♯)	b61⁴
	• Modulation to distant keys, e.g., F major b70, A♭ major b82.	

Texture and Instrument-ation	• Dramatic build-up of opening chord; Soprano only, joined by piano and harmonium, then by ATB.	b1–4
	• Homorhythmic SATB accompanied by tremolo piano chords and sustained harmonium chords.	b5–6
	• All parts descend in octaves to piano cadence.	b9⁴–17
	• Imitation between soli.	b34–39
	• Fugal texture.	b155–284
	• Sustained SATB chords accompanied by widely spaced piano and harmonium chords.	b306–314
Rhythm	• Fanfare-like dotted rhythms announce the opening *resurrexit* phrase.	b1–17
	• Semiquaver tremolo piano chords.	b155
	• Tempo is faster at the fugue with the change to 2/2 time.	b3–6
	• Counter-subject 2 is syncopated.	b162–169

11. *Preludio Religioso*

Background	It became common in France for the organist to play or improvise a piece during the Offertory, when the bread and wine are brought to the altar. Rossini intended this instrumental movement to be used for this purpose. It can be played as a piano solo or shared between the piano and harmonium. This piece also serves to demonstrate that despite writing little music since his retirement from opera, Rossini had kept a close eye on the latest developments in the Romantic style; the counterpoint and rich chromatic modulations were very reminiscent of the music being written at that time in Paris by the likes of César Franck and Gabriel Fauré.	
Structure and Tonality	Like many preludes, this has the feel of an improvisation based around 4 themes whose motifs are related to each other.	
	Introduction: F♯ minor, consisting mostly of solemn chromatic chords.	b1–16

	Section A: F# minor, the 4 themes are presented;	b17–69²
	• 1st theme, with an angular motif.	b17³–25¹
	• 2nd theme, a rising scalic figure.	b41–47¹
	• 3rd theme, derived from the 1st.	b47³–55
	• 4th theme, derived from the 1st and 2nd	b59–65¹
	Section A¹: C# minor, a modified repeat of the 4 themes.	b69³–113²
	Section A²: F# minor, based around the 1st theme only. Changes to tonic major at b145.	b113³–150
	Coda: a brief reminder of the Introduction chords, starting in a distant Bb minor, ending with an unusual final cadence Eb minor–F# major.	b151–154
Melody	• 1st theme – grows from the angular 4-note motif C#–D–F#–E#, which rises sequentially before changing to a descending arpeggio figure. Notice how the 4 notes of the implied C# minor cadence are a modified version of the initial motif (A–G#–B#–C#).	b17³–25¹
	• 2nd theme – a rising major scale on V of F# minor, which falls back to the tonic. This irregular 3-bar phrase is repeated a 4th higher.	b41–47¹
	• 3rd theme – the 3-note figure F#–G#–E is derived from the motif from the 1st theme. Treated as a long descending sequence.	b47³–55
	• 4th theme – the rising scale is taken from the 2nd theme, and a modified 4-note motif from the 1st can also be seen (RH, b60²⁻³ G#–A–B#–C#). Another 3-bar phrase like the 2nd.	b59–65¹
	• Section A¹ – 1st theme in LH is accompanied by a RH counter-melody, which is an inversion of the 4-note motif.	b69³–72
	• Section A² – the motif is briefly extended into a 2-bar sequential phrase ending with an appoggiatura. This phrase is gradually shortened to 4 notes from b119³, and 3 notes from b133³.	b113³–150

Harmony	• Although there is a clear sense of tonality running through the prelude, the harmony is very chromatic in the manner of Franck or Fauré, e.g., the opening chord progression: - b1 F#m - b2 G#dim/F# - b3 C#/E# - b4 German Augmented 6th on F • Tierce de Picardie chords. • Circle of 5ths using a variety of 7th chords. • Section A² – Franck-like sequence using a chain of French augmented 6ths, e.g., b119–120 (see below).	 b44 & 47 b48–51

	• Dominant pedal on C#. • Coda: starts with an unrelated B♭ minor chord, followed by an unusual final cadence E♭ minor–F# major.	b131–132 b151–154
Texture and Instrument-ation	A variety of textures and timbres can be seen in this movement: • Block **ff** piano chords in a darker low tessitura. • Contrasting **pp** chords played *una corda* in a higher tessitura. • Descending tritone figures in octaves. • 1st theme is presented in a 3-part fugal texture. • Close imitation between the parts can also be seen in the other themes, e.g., 2nd theme b41–47. • Parallel motion and contrary motion. • More homophonic towards the end. • Extreme and sudden dynamic contrasts, e.g., **ppp** and **ff** markings b119–end.	 b1–8 b9–12 b12⁴–16 b17–41 b28³–33 b127³
Rhythm	• Introduction and coda 4/4, main body 3/4. • Dramatic double-dotted rhythms. • 1st and 3rd themes start with an anacrusis, 2nd and 4th themes are syncopated, starting on the 2nd half of the 1st beat of the bar. • Heavy accents to reinforce climaxes.	 b1–12 b136–137

12. *Sanctus*

Background	A hymn of praise sung during the Eucharistic Prayer, the prayer used to bless the bread and wine for the communion.	

Structure	• The *Sanctus* is preceded by a short *ritornello* played by the harmonium (based on a phrase from b16–17 from the earlier *Gratias*), which establishes the tonic of C major.
	• The Sanctus itself is essentially strophic in form, with most of the same themes appearing in each verse, and a refrain on the words *Osanna in excelsis*:
	  - Verse 1
	  - Verse 2
	  - Verse 3 – extended with a new theme b42–56
		
		b1–17
		b18–34
		b35–61

Melody	5 main themes: • 1st theme (Soprano) – a fragmented rising C major arpeggio, followed by a descending conjunct figure. Chromatic passing note, F♯ b6^{4}. • 2nd theme (Bass) – a short motif that leaps up a perfect 5th before falling back in steps. • 3rd theme (soli) – the *Osanna* refrain, a rising arpeggic figure. • 4th theme (Soprano) – 8-bar question-and-answer phrase; after a rising major 6th (b18), a wave-shaped figure (b19) is varied (b20) before a C major cadence. The next 4 bars also begin with the rising major 6th, but then falls by step to a cadence in the dominant key G major. • 5th theme (Bass solo) – derived from a 5-note motif first heard in the 4th theme (b18^{6}–19^{4} D–C–E–F–G). • Final *Osanna* refrain is a combination of the 1st and 3rd themes.	b1–8 b8–9 b12^{6}–17 b18–25 b42–56 b56–61
Harmony and Tonality	• Tonality centred on C major, with modulations to more closely related keys compared with other movements, e.g., A minor b12, G major b25, C minor b42–46. • Tonal harmony, with some chromatic progressions, e.g., b46, key C minor: Cm–G7–A♭– dim 7th on E–F–aug 6th on A♭/F♯, leading to Ic–V^{7}–I in C major:	

	• Tonic pedal.	b18–21
	• Dominant pedal.	b27–29
	• Dissonant double suspension 9–8 and 4–3 (Soprano and Tenor).	b29
	• Final perfect cadence in C major chromatically decorated with C minor and C♯ dim triads.	b60
Texture and Instrument-ation	• A cappella setting for chorus and soli	
	• Contrary motion helps to develop the opening repeats of the word *Sanctus*.	b1–4
	• Frequent pedal points in the Bass, e.g., starting at b5, 18 and 27.	
	• Melody-dominated homophony.	b5–8
	• Imitation.	b8–10
	• Melody in octaves.	b12⁶–17
	• Divided Altos and Tenors to create 6-part harmony at the final climax.	b60–61
	• Very wide dynamic range near the end, from **ppp** b54 to **ff** b56.	
Rhythm	• 6/8 throughout.	
	• *Osanna* set in a fanfare-like speech rhythm, with 'san' stressed on the strongest beat of the bar.	b12⁶–13

13. O Salutaris

| **Background** | Written as an 'aria' for Soprano solo with piano accompaniment. The words are taken from a hymn that could be sung during the distribution of the bread and wine. They speak of the 'saving victim [Jesus] opening up the gates of heaven' and ask for 'help against surrounding enemies'. | |
| **Structure and Tonality** | Binary form with each section varied on its return, framed by an Introduction and a Coda. | |

	• Piano Introduction, tonic G major.	b1–20
	• A – G major, lyrical and expressive.	b21–44
	• B – more dramatic, modulates through a variety of keys, referring to 'enemies'.	b44–77
	• A^1 – G major, varied (e.g., G minor b86) and extended, developing ideas from the Introduction, e.g., b105–122.	b78–122
	• B^1 – a brief reprise.	b122–137
	• A^2 – G major, a repeat of b105–122.	b138–155
	• Coda, G major.	b155–174
Melody	Introduction:	
	• Opening 12-bar phrase built from a short rhythmic motif ♩ ♩ ♩ | ♪. ♪ ♪ which is developed both as a rising and falling sequence	b1–12
	• 2nd 8-bar phrase is arpeggic for 4 bars, followed by a climax on F natural, falling back down the scale to a perfect cadence in G major.	b13–20
	Section A:	
	• Opening Soprano melody has 2 x 8-bar question-and-answer phrases; each rises up the G major arpeggio to a climax on F♯, then falls back mostly by step, giving an arch-shape to both. The phrases differ in their tonality; the first stays mostly in the tonic whilst the second modulates first to B minor before cadencing in the dominant D major.	b21–36
	• Some Soprano melodies are taken from the piano Introduction, e.g., b37–44 and b93 onwards.	
	Section B:	
	• By contrast the phrases here are mostly on one note, and use enharmonic change to modulate, e.g., E♭–D♯.	b48–50
	• Descending chromatic scale, piano RH	b70–72
	Section A^1:	
	• Development of earlier Introduction themes:	
	- b13–14 extended as a rising sequence	b105–110
	- b5 extended as a descending sequence	b112–117
	• Section ends with a virtuoso G major arpeggio flourish spanning an 11th	b120–122
	Section B^1:	
	• Earlier monotone now rises chromatically to enhance the word-painting on *hostilia* (enemies).	b124–134

Harmony	• Contrast between the more tonal A sections and the tonally unstable B sections.	
	• Diminished 7th chords decorated with chromatic appoggiaturas (G♯, piano LH).	b13¹, 15¹
	• Tonality in A underlined by regular clear cadences, e.g., V–I in G b28–9, V–I in D b35–6.	
	• The tonal instability of B also enhances the word-painting on 'hostilia', which modulates freely through mediant keys E♭, B, and G major using enharmonic change.	b44–77
	• Chromatic harmony over dominant pedal D leading back to the tonic.	b70–77
	• Switching between tonic major (b78, 93) and minor (b86).	
	• Striking chain of dominant 7ths (e.g., B7 3rd inversion–G♯7–A7 3rd inversion).	b128–130
Texture and Instrumentation	• Melody-dominated homophony throughout.	
	• Detached, waltz-like piano accompaniment.	b21–36
	• Contrasting *ff* block chords in section B.	b46–56
	• Sudden change of dynamics to ***ppp***.	b58
Rhythm	• 3/4 throughout, with Section B more animated than A (word-painting on 'hostilia').	
	• Waltz style piano accompaniment.	b21–36
	• Accented syncopation in Soprano melody.	b24–26
	• Dramatic dotted/double dotted rhythms (Soprano, 'hostilia').	b49–50
	• Rhythms are busier at phrase endings, e.g., b120–122, ♩ movement replaced by ♪ s.	
	• 3/4 metre is displaced across the bar lines, e.g., piano RH phrasing b146²–153¹.	

14. Agnus Dei

Background	The text of the communion prayer *Agnus Dei* refers to Jesus as the sacrificial Lamb of God taking away the sins of the world. Rossini's setting, like many others, is solemn and reflective in mood with a more hopeful ending, although he also brings an operatic element to the Alto solo part and the climax near the end of the Mass as a whole.	
Structure and Tonality	Rossini uses the strophic structure outlined by the repetitive nature of the 3 lines of the text, with variety provided by the key scheme and melodic development:	
	• Introduction (tonic key E minor).	b1–7

	• A (E minor) Alto solo, followed by **a cappella** SATB response.	b8–20
	• A1 – as before, but with more modulation (E minor b21, C major b23, F minor b24, E♭ minor b31).	b21–32
	• A2 – as before, but modulating back to the tonic (E♭ minor b33, B major b35, E minor 36, C major b39, E minor b45).	b33–47
	• Coda (E minor/major) – 6-bar phrase with a $f\!f$ climax, cadencing in E minor. Repeated, but with a switch to E major. Finishes with a reprise of the Introduction.	b47–69
Melody	Section A: the Alto solo is a series of short phrases which are mostly derived from the first two phrases:	
	• a – auxiliary note figure B–C–B–C–B, followed by a descending tonic arpeggio in a semiquaver triplet with an F♯ appoggiatura.	b10^3–11^2
	• b – narrow range of a 4th, centred on E, mostly, ♩ and ♪ rhythms. The G♮ grace note forms a **false relation** with the piano G♯s.	b11^3–12^2
	• b^1 – same rhythm, but centred on A, and the range expanded to an octave.	b12^3–13^2
	• a^1 – auxiliary note figure is varied.	b13^3–14^2
	• a^2 – closer to the original rhythm of a.	b14^3–15^2
	• a^3 – auxiliary note figure is rhythmically augmented.	b15^3–17^2
	• c – a demanding opera-style **coloratura** phrase that outlines the Ic–V–I cadence in E minor with some chromatic ornaments, e.g., A♯ appoggiatura b$18^{3.}$	b17^3–19^1
	• Chorus Soprano part has a contrasting simple, mostly stepwise melody, which is treated sequentially	b19–20
	• The coloratura phrase c covers a wider range when repeated, e.g., diminished 12th b30.	
	• The ♩ and ♪ the rhythms of b are developed and extended later on.	b37^3–43^2
Harmony and Tonality	• Tonally centred on E minor/major, but visits a range of distant keys, e.g., E♭ minor b31.	
	• Tonic pedal.	b8–11
	• Rich chromatic chord progressions, e.g.:	b50^4–53^1
	- Dim 7th on E b50^4	
	- Dim 7th on D♯ b51^1	
	- Augmented 6th on E♭ b51^2	
	- G minor/D b51^3	
	- Augmented 6th on D♯ then C b51^4	

	- Ic of E minor b52[1] - V minor 9th (B–D♯–F♯–A–C) b52[3] - I of E minor b53[1] (see below) • Diatonic harmony (a cappella SATB). • Neapolitan 6th in E minor (A–C–F♮).	b19–20 b17[3]
Texture and Instrument-ation	• Alto solo, SATB chorus, piano and harmonium. • Demanding Alto solo, ranging a 15th. • Alto solos are melody-dominated homophony. • Accompaniment similar to that of the opening *Kyrie*; the piano plays detached syncopated chords over LH octaves, whilst the harmonium doubles the piano with contrasting sustained chords. • **a cappella** homophonic choral texture. • Counterpoint between the vocal parts in the Coda.	 b19–20 b47–50
Rhythm	• Common time, with a slow ♪ pulse resulting in the use of shorter note values. • Syncopated demisemiquavers and semiquavers (32nd and 16th notes) throughout the *Agnus Dei* sections, RH piano. • Most of the Alto solo phrases are placed across the bar line. • Semiquaver triplets (Alto solo) create a cross-rhythm with the semiquavers in piano RH. • Hemidemisemiquaver (64th note) tremolo reinforce the *ff* climaxes, piano RH. • Unpredictable fragmented rhythms in the piano Introduction and ending.	 b8–44 b10[3]–11[2] b11[1] b52, 58 b1–7, 62–69

Sample questions

In Section A of the examination there will be one question on each of the two prescribed works. You must choose to answer **one** of these **two** questions (as well as a third 'musical links' question that will be discussed later). Here are four sample questions based on the *Petite messe solennelle* to use for practice. You may answer these in continuous prose or detailed bullet points, and you should allow around 30 minutes under timed conditions to complete each question.

Reference should be made to an unmarked copy of the score and remember to give precise locations for the musical features you discuss.

1. In what ways can Rossini's *Petite messe solennelle* be thought of as a typical 19th-century Romantic work?
2. Compare and contrast **two** different choral movements from the *Petite messe solennelle* and write informatively about both.
3. Discuss Rossini's approach to melody writing in *Petite messe solennelle*. Refer to **at least two** different movements in your answer.
4. Discuss Rossini's use of harmony and tonality in *Petite messe solennelle*. Refer to **at least two** different movements in your answer.

AN AMERICAN IN PARIS (1928) – GEORGE GERSHWIN

Context

There are some interesting parallels between Gioachino Rossini and George Gershwin. Both had hugely successful careers composing for the theatre, and both possessed an amazing facility for melody writing. Unusually for someone who started out writing songs for New York's Tin Pan Alley, Gershwin also found success in the concert hall with *Rhapsody in Blue* and *Concerto in F*, both for piano and orchestra. He enjoyed several visits to Paris during the 1920s and was inspired to compose another orchestral piece based on his impressions of the city. Whilst he was there Gershwin met many of his early 20th-century contemporaries: composers such as Ravel, Stravinsky, Prokofiev, Poulenc and Milhaud. Not surprisingly you will hear a strong modern French influence, particularly the Impressionist style pioneered by Debussy, which Gershwin combined with American Blues and Jazz elements. One of the impressions that stuck in Gershwin's mind was the sound of the Parisian taxi horns and, instead of trying to replicate them in the piece with orchestral instruments alone, he bought some of the taxi horns and added them to the percussion section in his score.

An American in Paris is a **tone poem**, a descriptive genre of music from the 19th century in which a 'programme' explaining the composer's intended images or story was added to the score. Gershwin's own (deliberately general) programme describes an American walking the streets of Paris absorbing the sights and sounds of the city, but then feeling homesick for a while, before once again revelling in the Parisian atmosphere. A more detailed programme for the piece was written by Deems Taylor, another American composer of that time, and his version is particularly useful for analysing the structure and the themes. Locations using bar numbers are based on the Alfred full miniature score.

Structure	There are 681 bars in total, and the piece can be thought of as a **Binary form** (AB) with a coda:	
	A – Walking around the streets of Paris, taking in the sights and sounds of the city. The music here is influenced by early 20th century French music. Themes are presented as follows:	b1–391
	• A1 – 1st Walking theme, oboe and violins.	b1–8
	• A2 – Taxi horn theme.	b28–59
	• *La Sorella* theme, a popular French tune written by Charles Borel-Clerc in 1905, quoted briefly by Gershwin in the trombones.	b96–100
	• A3 – 2nd Walking theme, clarinets.	b119–126
	• Development of the 2 Walking/Taxi themes.	b152–248
	• A4 – 3rd Walking theme,(or 'Left Bank' theme according to Taylor), trumpets, trombones and 1st violins.	b251–282
	• A5 – for solo violin (Taylor suggests the man has been approached by a young lady). Answered by brief reprise of A1 in the cor anglais.	b362–365
	B – The character suddenly feels homesick, which is reflected in the central Blues theme and the Jazz theme that follows.	b392–591
	• B1 – the homesick Blues theme, which is central to the whole piece. First heard on solo trumpet.	b396–407
	• B2 – a Jazz-style theme, solo trumpet, then trombone.	b481–493
	• A reprise of B1 brings the section to a close.	b564
	Coda – the Parisian spirit returns and the homesickness is forgotten as themes from both sections are reprised and combined for a grand finale:	b592–681
	• A1, woodwind.	b592
	• A5, flute, then clarinet.	b604
	• A4, brass with a variant of A3, xylophone and violins.	b612
	• A2, taxi horns and trombones with A3, violins.	b629
	• A3 (flute/violin) with A1 (bassoon, trombone, tuba, lower strings).	b635
	• A3 (oboes, horns) with A4 (flutes, clarinet, trumpets, upper strings).	b649
	• A final reprise of B1 with variants of A3 for full orchestra.	b665–end

Melody	Themes:	
	• A1 – F major, **diatonic**, a cheerful 8-bar melody built from a 3-note angular motif C–D–E, decorated with a B♮ grace note.	
	(b1). This motif is repeated and developed b2–6, and followed by another motif with distinctive repeated semiquaver E's, which is important later on. Tonic note F does not appear until the final note.	
	• A2 – the noise of the taxi horns is represented by a tritone leap D♭–G b29–30, which later becomes an augmented 5th D♭–A b37–8.	
	These two intervals are heard alternately to imply a **whole-tone scale** b40–3.	
	• A3 – B♭ major, another jaunty Walking theme. 8 bars, clearly divided into 4 x 2-bar units, all using the repeated semiquaver E's motif in A1 b7:	
	1. Repeated high B♭s leap up to a D and down a tritone to an A♭. Decorated with a glissando at the start.	b119–120
	2. A descending sequence of 119–20.	b121–122
	3. As 119–20.	b122–123
	4. A chromatic variant cadencing on B♭.	b123–124
	• A4 – E major, **Binary** phrase structure AA¹BB¹ with irregular phrase lengths:	
	- A – 9 bars, narrow range of a perfect 5th, built on a mostly stepwise 2-bar motif that is repeated before rising to a long-held F♯	b251–259
	- A¹ – 9 bars, as A but ending on F double sharp	b260–268
	- B – 6 bars, same range as A, cadences on G♯ minor, entirely stepwise with repeated D♯s mid-phrase	b269–274
	- B¹ – 8 bars, as B but finishing a tone lower on F♯	b275–282
	• A5 – outlines the underlying dominant 9th chord of F major, a theme that rises up a C major arpeggio, then descends in a wave shape using a semiquaver triplet figure	b362–365
	• B1 – B♭ major, 12-bar Blues phrase structure AA¹B:	
	- A – 4 bars, starting on a high semibreve F before descending in mostly stepwise quavers to F an octave below. D♭ (written E♭) b397³ is a **blue note**. The final long-held F is a typical Blues feature, during which a counter-melody is heard in the flutes	b396–399

	- A^1 – 4 bars, as A but ending on the tonic. Responding counter-melody, flutes, bass clarinet and violas	b400–403
	- B – Starts with an appoggiatura, followed by a series of falling chromatic phrases (including 2 more blue notes b405³) before cadencing on the tonic	b404–407
	• B2 – D major, 12-bar Blues (3 x 4) phrase structure based on an angular arpeggio figure:	
	- A – Entirely arpeggic on D major, wide range of 2 octaves. Jazz-style syncopation b483	b481⁴–485
	- A^1 – G major arpeggio, followed by a repeated trill figure that uses a blue note (sounds as an F♮ b487)	b485⁴–489
	- A^2 – broken octaves on A and E, followed by longer syncopation (trumpet, then trombone)	b489⁴–493
	Melodic development: like Debussy, Gershwin continuously develops his themes throughout the whole piece. Here a just a few examples:	
	A1 – 1st Walking theme.	
	• The ♪♪♪ ♪♪ figure (b7) is passed around the brass section and then shortened to create a 3/8 cross rhythm against the 2/4 metre (horns/strings).	b20–26
	• Augmentation, violins.	b186–190
	• Descending sequence, bass instruments.	b195–201
	• Augmentation of the repeated semiquavers, full brass, upper strings near the end.	b675–676
	A3 – 2nd Walking theme.	
	• Chromatic figure (b125–126) repeated as a rising sequence (upper woodwind/strings).	b132–135
	• Main 2-bar motif passed around the orchestra with extra semiquavers/demisemiquavers added.	b178–185
	• Variant in horns used in counterpoint with A4.	b283–297
	A4 – 3rd Walking theme.	
	• Heard in augmentation with mysterious parallel **bitonal** chords.	b369²–372
	B1 – Homesick Blues theme.	
	• Descending quaver blue note figure (b397) repeated as a descending sequence, diminution to semiquavers	b461–464
	• A variant of (b397) using a rising Blues scale on D (oboe/cor anglais)	b516–523
	• b397 appears again at the end of the piece (lower woodwind/alto saxophone)	b677–678
	B2 – Jazz-style theme	
	• Final appearance of this theme fragments into ever-shorter repeats of the broken octaves figure (woodwind/timpani/strings)	b541–555

Harmony and Tonality	Gershwin uses a variety of traditional and modern harmonic styles, showing the diversity of the piece:	
	• Non-functional harmony on F major under the 1st Walking theme; there is no cadence to confirm the key. Shows the influence of Debussy.	b1–10
	• 1st Walking theme later harmonized with parallel chromatic major triads, creating dissonance (D–F♯–E–G–B♭–A–A♭–G–G♭–F). Another Debussy influence.	b16–20
	• The brief appearance of *La Sorella* is diatonic harmony in F♯ major, but unrelated major triads soon reappear (G and B♭, horns and upper strings b101–104).	b97–104
	• 2nd Walking theme – tonic-dominant harmony in B♭ major, with a mediant modulation to D♭ major b136.	b119–126
	• Rich Jazz chord extensions:	
	- $F^{7\sharp 11}$ (F–A–E♭–G–B♮)	b149^2
	- $E^{7\sharp 11}$ (E–G♯–D–F♯–A♯)	b150^1
	- C^9 (C–E–G–B♭–D)	b360–369
	• Further Impressionist non-functional harmony, with extended parallel chords moving in contrary motion.	b204–219
	• A sense of tonality is maintained with tonic and dominant pedals:	
	- In E major, dominant B–tonic E, in the Bass	b239–255
	- Near the end in F major, dominant C–tonic F, in the Bass	b641–663
	• Tonic triads are sometimes avoided by replacing the third with a suspended 4th, e.g., key E major, but first chord is E–A–B.	b283
	• Clear cadences are rare, but there is an implied Vb–I in G♯ minor (G♮ instead of F double sharp, cello).	b272–273
	• **Bitonal** (two different chords sounding at the same time) harmonic progression shows the influence of Stravinsky and Poulenc:	
	- C major/F♯ major	b369^2
	- G♯ major/D major	b370^1
	- F major/B major, (etc.)	b370^2
	• B1 – homesick Blues theme features a repeated 2-bar progression centred on B♭ major, with most of the basic triads chromatically altered and/or extended in the Jazz style:	b392–401
	- b392; B♭–G$^{7\sharp 5\flat 9}$ (G–C♭–E♭–F–A♭)	
	- b393; Cm^7–B♭^{6}/D–E♭m^6–F^{13} (see below)	

Bb   G7(b9#5)   Cm7 Bbb6/D Ebm6   F13

- perfect cadence in the tonic	b405–406
• B2 uses the outline of a 12-bar Blues progression in D with Jazz extensions and additions:	b481–493

- D⁷ | D⁷ | D⁷ | D⁷ |
- G⁷ | Gm | Gm | F#m⁷, E⁷ |
- A⁷ | A⁷ | D | D |

- • In the Coda the outline of a **circle of 5ths** can be traced through the following tonal centres:
  - A, b592–609
  - D, b610–613
  - G, b614–634
  - C, b635–644
  - F, b645–663

Texture and Instrument-ation	• Gershwin scored this piece for a large orchestra, to which he added alto, tenor and baritone saxophones that add an authentic Blues/Jazz sound.	
	• Parisian taxi horns are recreated by combining real taxi horns with closed French horns (that is, the bell is totally shut off by the player's hand) and glissandi in strings and woodwind.	b40–43
	• Themes are frequently accompanied both by bass/ chords and counter-melodies, e.g., 1st Walking theme has counter-melodies in flutes/oboes, bassoon/2nd violin/viola.	b12–15
	• Trumpets use a variety of mutes to alter their sound, including the 'felt crown' in the homesick Blues theme, a mute made by Jazz musicians by cutting the rim from a fedora hat.	b395
	• **Call and response**; the Blues theme is answered at the end of each phrase, e.g., flutes b399.	
	• The strings are used in a wide variety of ways:	
	- 'sul G', using the darker low register of the violins	b28
	- *Near the frog*' (strings) means play at the heel end of the bow, giving a more percussive attack to the sound	b32
	- Tremolo (violins b106–9)	
	- Divisi (viola/cello b174)	
	- Artificial harmonics (violins b170)	
	- With mutes (*con sordini*)	b201
	- Double stopping	b283–287
	- Switching between pizzicato and arco	b283–301
	- Portamento (upper strings b517–518)	

	• Glissandi in violins, and shared between clarinets and flutes (oboe later).	b324–337
	• Bass drum / snare drum / cymbals are sometimes used as a drum kit, e.g., b417 and b494–503.	
	• Build-up of ostinato patterns across the orchestra to a climax in the Coda.	b612–663
	• Contrary motion.	b204–211

Rhythm	A number of typical 20th-century rhythmic features can be heard:	
	• The ♪♪♪♪ ♪♪ motif (b7) is passed around the brass section and then shortened to create a 3/8 cross-rhythm against the 2/4 metre (horns/strings). It is also used in a modified form at the opening of the 2nd Walking theme (b119 clarinet).	b20–26
	• Cross-rhythms:	
	- 3/8 (flute/xylophone), 3/4 (bassoon/ cello/bass) and 2/4 (horns/upper strings) patterns play at the same time	b32–35
	- 4/4 Blues theme is accompanied by syncopated 3/8 chords	b564–71
	• Polyrhythm – a variety of quaver, semiquaver, quaver triplet and crotchet triplet rhythms are all heard simultaneously.	b174–194
	• Changing metres, e.g., 3/4, 5/4, 4/4, 3/4, 2/4.	b208–212
	• Syncopation, trumpet solo b482^4–483. 4/4 metre also disrupted by 3+3+2 cross-rhythm emphasised by trills, trumpet b487–488.	

Sample questions

In Section A of the examination there will be one question on each of the two prescribed works. You must choose to answer **one** of these **two** questions (as well as a third 'musical links' question that will be discussed later). Here are four sample questions based on *An American in Paris* to use for practice. You may answer these in continuous prose or detailed bullet points and you should allow around 30 minutes under timed conditions to complete each question. Reference should be made to an unmarked copy of the score and remember to give precise locations for the musical features you discuss.

1. Gershwin once described *An American in Paris* as 'the most modern music I've yet attempted'. In what ways can *An American in Paris* be thought of as a typical early 20th-century work?
2. *An American in Paris* draws upon musical elements from both Western European and American cultures. Identify **two (or more)** elements that have

roots in Western European music and **two (or more)** elements that originate from American music. Discuss how these elements contribute to the
overall style of the work.

3. Discuss Gershwin's handling of tonality and harmony in *An American in
   Paris*. Refer in detail to specific passages of music.

4. Discuss Gershwin's handling of texture and orchestration in *An American in
   Paris*. Refer in detail to specific passages of music.

LINKS BETWEEN THE PRESCRIBED WORKS (HL ONLY)

Question 3 requires HL candidates to compare and contrast the *Petite messe
solennelle* and *An American in Paris* with regard to one or two musical elements or
concepts. This means you must write about similarities and differences in the
use of, for example, melody and rhythm between the prescribed works, taking
care to ensure your points are relevant to the elements or concepts asked in
the question. For example, in a question about Instrumentation, while it is true
to state that both works contain keyboard instruments, this is not a significant
musical link; but a comparative discussion of *how keyboard instruments are used in
each work* is creditworthy in the IB examination.

The following is a list of some of the musical links between the *Petite messe
solennelle* and *An American in Paris*, along with the locations of possible examples
(you will of course need to add your own explanations – a useful revision task):

Comparative:

- Both works contain mostly diatonic melodies with some chromaticism (*Pms*
  Domine Deus b18–53, *AAiP* b119–26).
- Syncopated phrase openings (*Pms* Quoniam b48^4–55, *AAiP* b251–259).
- The altered 3rd in a false relation (*Pms* Agnus Dei b23^1 Alto D♯) can be
  compared with the blue note (*AAiP* b397^3).
- Themes developed sequentially from motifs (*Pms* Domine Deus b1–16, *AAiP*
  b119–126).
- Appoggiaturas (*Pms* Crucifixus b19^1, *AAiP* b404^1).
- Grace notes/acciaccaturas (*Pms* Agnus Dei b1–3, *AAiP* b1–6).
- Glissandi (*Pms* O Salutaris b162 and 170, *AAiP* b119).
- Augmentation of a theme (*Pms* Gratias b106–114, *AAiP* b186–190, violins).
- Question-and-answer phrasing (*Pms* Domine Deus b18–33, *AAiP* b119–126).
- Binary form (*Pms* Gloria-Laudamus, *AAiP* A b1, B b392, coda b592).
- Both works use link passages as dominant preparation for the following sec-
  tion or movement (*Pms* Domine Deus b151–164, *AAiP* b239–248).
- Tonal centres defined by perfect cadences (*Pms* Domine Deus b52–53, *AAiP*
  b405–406).

- Dominant pedal points (*Pms* Et Resurrexit b252–267, *AAiP* b381–391).
- Mediant modulations (*Pms* Crucifixus Ab major to Et Resurrexit B major, *AAiP* Bb major to Db major b136).
- Switches from tonic major to minor (*Pms* Domine Deus D major–minor b18–26, *AAiP* Bb major–minor b406–409).
- Dominant 9th chords (*Pms* Kyrie D⁹ b27¹, *AAiP* C⁹ b360).
- Chromatic harmonic sequences (*Pms* Preludio Religioso b119–123, *AAiP* b239–248).
- Ostinato chordal textures (*Pms* Gloria-Laudamus b25 onwards, *AAiP* b1–10).
- Melody-dominated homophony (*Pms* Quoniam b29–36, *AAiP* b392–398).
- Imitation (*Pms* Gratias b76–80, *AAiP* b583–586).
- Counterpoint (*Pms* Cum Sancto Spiritu b26 onwards, *AAiP* b665–668).
- Polyrhythm (*Pms* Domine Deus b123–33, *AAiP* b564–571).
- Syncopated chordal accompaniment (*Pms* Crucifixus, *AAiP* b392–403).

Contrasting:

- Both works stray a long way from the tonic, but using different means (*Pms* uses chromatic modulations, for example, Cum Sancto Spiritu Gb major b149–152, *AAiP* disrupts the sense of key with, for example, bitonal passages b369–372).
- Both works contain a lot of chromatic harmony, but *Pms* uses it to colour what is still a tonal work with regular clear cadences. *AAiP* is also regarded as a tonal work, but Gershwin often uses chromatic harmony in the manner of Debussy to weaken the sense of key, that is, purely for effect, and avoids clear cadences.

Sample Questions

In Section A (question 3) of the examination there will be one compulsory question linking both the *Petite messe solennelle* and *An American in Paris*. Here are three to use for practice. You may answer these in continuous prose or detailed bullet points and you should allow around 30 minutes to complete each question. Reference should be made to unmarked copies of both scores and remember to give precise locations for the musical features you discuss.

1. Investigate significant musical links between these two pieces by analysing and comparing their use of texture and rhythm.
2. *Petite messe solennelle* and *An American in Paris* were both composed in Paris and only 65 years apart. Referring to both works, comment on the musical features they have in common.
3. Compare and contrast the ways tonality and harmony are used in both works.

PRESCRIBED WORKS 2017–19

BRANDENBURG CONCERTO NO. 2 IN F MAJOR BWV 1047 (c.1719–21) – J. S. BACH

Introduction

This Prescribed Work is the second of a set of 6 concertos scored for a variety of instrumental combinations that Johann Sebastian Bach sent to Christian-Ludwig, Margrave of Brandenburg–Schwedt in 1721. Concerto no. 2 is believed to have been composed in or around 1719. The Margrave had asked Bach to send him some of his compositions, and it is most likely all 6 concertos were written during the period Bach was employed as *Kapellmeister* to the prince of Anhalt-Cöthen. Indeed, most of Bach's chamber and orchestral music dates from his time in this post.

These concertos are mostly of a type called *concerto grosso* (literally *big concert*), a popular genre among middle to late Baroque composers, including Corelli, Vivaldi, Handel and of course Bach. A concerto grosso features two contrasting instrumental groups; the **concertino**, a smaller group of soloists, and the **ripieno**, the tutti or full orchestra (usually strings). Both of these groups were accompanied by the **continuo**, which is heard in almost all Baroque music, most commonly a harpsichord and cello, which provided the harmonic filling and bass line respectively. Whilst both groups would have shared some of the same musical material, other themes were played exclusively by the concertino. Furthermore, the part writing for the concertino group was usually more virtuosic and elaborate.

Bach was known as an experimenter, which can be seen in this work, with its unusual concertino group of tromba, (treble) recorder, oboe and violin, his often novel approach to musical structures, and his daring use of harmony and dissonance.

Instrumentation

The 'tromba' referred to by Bach in his score was a natural trumpet in high F, with no valves, which meant it played only the notes of the harmonic series.

The sound of the tromba in the 18th century was softer in both timbre and dynamic compared to a modern trumpet, which explains why Bach was able to use it in a concertino group alongside a treble recorder, oboe and violin without any problems with balance. The solo tromba part Bach wrote was at one time regarded as unplayable because of technical difficulties and tuning issues on certain harmonics. It is likely he had a particular performer in mind for this part, since virtuoso trumpet and horn players would travel around Europe and were highly sought after. But with research into Baroque performance techniques and construction leading to the development of the so-called Baroque Trumpet, these problems have been overcome and many fine recordings of this work have been made since.

Bach's score also calls for a violone in the ripieno strings. The violone was a name given to a variety of lower stringed instruments, but it is most likely he intended the part to be played by one of the larger double bass viols, similar in size to the modern double bass. Like the double bass, the violone sounds an octave lower than written, therefore adding real depth to the sound of the orchestra.

1st movement

Context	A lively opening movement in the concerto grosso style. Although Bach gave a 2/2 time signature there is no tempo indication; the movement is usually played at a moderate tempo with a 4/4 crotchet pulse.
Themes and Motifs	The 8-bar main tutti Ritornello theme is built from four 2-bar motifs, each starting with an **anacrusis** on the upbeat: 1. 1st tutti motif b1 (see below): outlining a tonic F major triad with B♭ passing notes, with a rising **dactylic** ♪.♪♪ rhythm. Repeated in b2.  2. 2nd tutti motif bb3-4 consists of mostly conjunct semiquavers. 3. 3rd tutti motif bb5-6 – derived from the 1st motif, once again outlining the tonic triad with passing notes, but now with a falling dactylic pattern. 4. 4th tutti motif bb7-8 – similar to the 2nd in rhythm. Mostly semiquavers outlining the tonic and dominant 7th chords, before a cadence in the tonic decorated with a trill.

5. An additional tutti motif (bb1-2) can also be heard in the bass parts as a counterpoint to the 1st motif; it revolves conjunctly around the tonic F mostly in semiquavers.

There are also two additional concertino themes (again both anacrusic) used exclusively by the soloists:

6. bb9-10 – *1st concertino theme*, heard in the violin to begin with, rises in steps to the tonic with a trill on the leading note E before dropping an octave and becoming more arpeggic in nature.

7. bb32-35 – *2nd concertino theme*, a quaver motif played in imitation, initially between the tromba and the oboe. It is taken from the C-F-C quavers in the 1st tutti motif (b1$^{3-4}$ upper parts).

Structure and Tonality	118 bars, F major, in **ritornello form** with the main *tutti* motifs returning in different combinations in a variety of related keys between *episodes* for the four soloists, who have their own additional exclusive themes. • bb1-8 – opening tutti in F major. • bb9-22 – 1st episode, modulates to the dominant (C major). Each soloist presents the 1st concertino theme, with 2-bar tutti interjections in between. • bb23-28 – shortened 2nd tutti in C major (6 bars). • bb29-35 – 2nd episode in F major, moving towards D minor. Tromba reprises 1st concertino theme, and then presents the 2nd in imitation with the oboe. • bb36-39 – 3rd tutti in D minor (4 bars). • bb40-55 – 3rd episode, developing the tutti motifs, starting from D minor and moving through two harmonic sequences (circle of 5ths followed by a 3 x 2-bar sequence of dominant 7ths towards B♭ major. • bb56-59 – 4th tutti in B♭ major (4 bars), with the opening motif in the bass for 2 bars. • bb60-67 – 4th episode featuring the 1st concertino theme, moving towards C minor. • bb68-71 – 5th tutti in C minor. • bb72-79 – 5th episode, featuring the 2nd concertino theme b76, moving towards G minor. • bb80-83 – 6th tutti in G minor. • bb84-102 – 6th episode, moving through D minor and A minor. Further thematic development (e.g., 1st tutti motif in double canon soli b94). • bb103-118 – final tutti in F major, with a restatement of all the tutti motifs, briefly interrupted by the 3 x 2-bar sequence of dominant 7ths heard earlier (b107).

Melodic Development	Bach is highly creative with the many ways in which he juggles his motifs: • Motifs in **counterpoint**, e.g., 1st and 5th tutti motifs, b1 upper parts and bass. This 5th bass motif is later heard in the tromba above the 1st (b19). • 2nd concertino theme b32³ is accompanied by the ripieno bass playing part of the 2nd tutti motif in a circle of 5ths sequence. • 5th tutti motif in **contrary motion** (recorder/oboe/violin) as the tromba plays the 1st (b40). • Bach '**spins out**' (German = *fortspinnung*) the 3rd tutti motif between the soloists, above a chromatic harmonic sequence of dominant 7th chords, leading to the same motif appearing in the ripieno bass in B♭ major (bb50-57). • **Extra notes** added to the 1st tutti motif (D, bb86-87 solo violin). • 1st tutti motif in **canon** (bb87-88 ripieno bass leading off, followed by tromba 2 beats after). This is followed up later by a double canon for the soloists (b93⁴ recorder/violin in 6ths, tromba/oboe in 3rds 2 beats after).

Harmony	• bb1-8 – entirely **diatonic**, mostly primary triads in root position and 1st inversion, with a Ic-V-I perfect cadence b8.
	   ◦ **Dissonance** results from passing notes and auxiliary notes (b3 recorder/oboe/violin)
	   ◦ Accented passing notes decorating the cadence mentioned above (b8 B♭ over the F major chord resolving to the A, recorder/oboe/violin)
	• Continuo bass part also decorated with passing notes, e.g., b9² (A) and b9⁴ (G).
	• Modulations to related keys confirmed by perfect cadences, e.g., dominant C major b28, relative minor (D) b39.
	• bb32-36 – complete **circle of 5ths** starting and ending on D minor chord. This is most clearly seen in the violone part.
	• There are also some **chromatic** chords and progressions:
	   ◦ 2-bar sequence of dominant 7ths:
	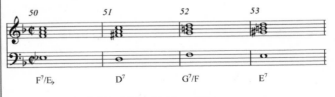
	   ◦ b112 – diminished 7th chord on B♮
	• b64 recorder – chain of 9-8 **suspensions.**

Below the music notation: 50, 51, 52, 53

F⁷/E♭   D⁷   G⁷/F   E⁷

Texture	A wide variety of textures abound in this movement, polyphonic in the main supported by the ripieno and continuo parts filling in the harmony.
	• bb1-2 – two of the ritornello motifs are heard in **counterpoint** together in the upper parts and the cello/violone.
	• bb9-22 – contrast in textures between solo passages with continuo and alternating tutti interjections.
	• bb32³-35 – 2nd concertino theme heard in antiphonal **imitation** (tromba and oboe) with the following accompaniments:
	○ **Double-stopped** solo violin
	○ Counterpoint from the ritornello bass theme first heard in bb1-2 played in parallel 3rds (recorder and continuo)
	○ Ripieno violins play sustained notes to fill in the harmony and bind the other independent lines together
	• bb50-55 – a more homophonic accompaniment can be heard underneath the soloists' polyphony:
	○ Detached chords, ripieno strings
	○ Repeated cello/violone bass notes
	○ Ripieno 1st violin outlines the harmony in syncopated crotchets
	• bb70-71 – **antiphonal** octave G's between upper and lower ripieno strings/continuo.
	• b87⁴ – **canon** between violone/continuo and tromba half a bar later.
	• b93⁴ – double canon between recorder/violin and tromba/oboe, each pair moving in **parallel motion**.
	• b102⁴ – 1st ritornello motif heard in **unison** across all parts including the continuo harpsichord ('**tasto solo**' = play the notes with no chords).
Rhythm	• The time signature is 'cut time' which usually means 2 minims in a bar. However, Bach does not give a tempo marking, and most performances given today have a moderate 4 in a bar pulse.
	• The continuo cello and violone parts move mostly in quavers and semiquavers, which drives the music onwards with purpose.
	• The 1st and 3rd ritornello motifs both feature dactylic rhythmic patterns (i.e., long-short-short).
	• All of the thematic material is anacrusic, starting with an upbeat.
	• Syncopated crotchet accompaniment (bb50-55 ripieno 1st violin).

2nd movement: Andante

Context	A calm and expressive Andante in the relative minor to contrast with the more vigorous outer movements. The tromba and ripieno strings do not play here, leaving a more intimate chamber-like ensemble of recorder, oboe, violin and continuo.
Structure and Tonality	65 bars, a fugal discussion of two simple melodic ideas. Although the continuo never plays either of these melodies and remains in its role as the accompanist, the three solo parts bear many of the hallmarks of a fugue as outlined below. • bb1-7 – Exposition, D minor. The violin announces the fugue **subject**, followed immediately by real answers in the tonic from the oboe and recorder. During these answers the **countersubject** is introduced (violin bb3³-5¹, oboe bb5³-7¹). • bb8-23 – Episode, during which the key moves through A minor and cadences in C major. The subject is developed in a series of new variants. • bb23³-33 – Middle Entries, in C major and modulating to B♭ major. The subject is varied again in the violin and recorder, but the oboe restates the original in a brief return to the tonic (b27³). • bb33-37 – Brief episode where the countersubject is varied and passed around the soloists in a **circle of 5ths**. • bb37³-43 – Middle entries in G minor. • bb43³-57 – Episode, starting with the oboe playing a subject variant from b7³ in the tonic, before an extended discussion of the countersubject across a complete circle of 5ths ending on V of D minor. • bb57³-65 – Final entries in the tonic first in the violin, followed by the oboe. The last recorder entry is an extended cadential version of the subject, ending on a **tierce de Picardie** b65.
Melodic Development	Bach skilfully makes the most of his two simple melodic ideas: **Subject** • Mostly conjunct, narrow range of a minor 6th, anacrusic, diatonic, **anapaestic** rhythmic figure (b2³), decorated at the end with a trill and an accented passing note (E, b3²).

Countersubject

- Also mostly conjunct and anacrusic. Two short falling figures, which are either a suspension or an appoggiatura; the second is a decorated descending sequence of the first.
- The opening F-F-E figure was originally heard in the 1st movement (bb63⁴-65, recorder) and could be thought of as a motif that unifies the concerto as a whole.
- Notice how the use of crotchet rests contrasts with the subject and creates holes in the texture so that each part can be heard more clearly.

Several variants of both the subject and the countersubject can be heard as the movement progresses.

Subject

- b7³ recorder – now in A minor, the first quaver is replaced by two semiquavers. Also note the expressive falling diminished 4th C-G# b8³. Heard again in the tonic later (b43³ oboe).
- b9³ oboe – the first interval in the anapaestic figure is widened to a perfect 5th, and the crotchet from b3¹ is replaced by two quavers forming an additional accented passing note in a descending scale.
- b13³ recorder – a shorter cadential variant ending more decisively as a crotchet on the first beat of the bar.
- b23³ violin – the rhythm of b3 has been elaborated with two dactylic patterns. Imitated by the recorder two bars later.
- b61³ recorder – extended to a 4-bar phrase by repeating the anapaestic figure before cadencing on the tonic, decorated with an anticipation b64³.

Countersubject

- b7¹ violin – instead of falling, the appoggiatura rises to the tonic.
- b19³ oboe/violin – played in parallel 3rds.
- b33² oboe – starts one beat earlier with an additional crotchet. This variant is passed around the soloists in a circle of 5ths sequence with parallel 3rds and 6ths.
- b50³ – a series of sequential double suspensions passed between the soloists in pairs.

The continuo cello line maintains a harmonic outline in quavers, stopping only for important cadences.

Harmony	• largely diatonic, with modulations confirmed by cadences, e.g., Ic-V-I in A minor bb14-15.
	• however, cadence points like this also contain dissonance resulting from the polyphonic lines of the soloists:
	  ○ Parallel 9ths (b14 oboe and continuo cello)
	  ○ The violin C at the end of b14 clashes with the E major chord played by the continuo harpsichord
	  ○ The A minor chord on the next beat (b15^1) has two accented passing notes running through it (oboe and violin in 3rds) before briefly resolving onto harmony notes
	• Circle of 5ths sequence – a complete circle can be traced, starting and ending on A (bb49-56 cello).
	• Interrupted cadence V-VI in D minor bb62-63 helps to extend the final phrase by delaying the expected perfect cadence.
	• Hemiola bb63-64 reinforced by two striking diminished 7th chords on B♭ and B♮, before resolving to the final Ic-V-I cadence in D minor.
	• Tierce de Picardie on the final tonic chord b65.

Rhythm	• 3/4 time throughout, Andante. • Almost continuous cello quavers push the movement along, with cadences marked by crotchets. • Anapaestic rhythm ♪♪♩ in the fugue subject (b2^3). • The subject and countersubject both start with an anacrusis. • **Hemiola** bb63-64, most clearly seen in the cello part.
Texture	• Fugal texture for the soloists, with harmonic support from the continuo cello and harpsichord. • Canonic imitation of the fugue subject (bb1-7 soloists). • Parallel motion (b12 oboe and violin in 3rds). • Contrary motion (bb50-54 soloists' imitation of the countersubject in pairs)

3rd movement: Allegro assai

Context	This movement resembles the 1st movement in many ways; vigorous energy, and similar thematic and rhythmic material cast in a ritornello form in F major. However, the ripieno strings' role is very much reduced, given that they are silent for the first 46 bars, and when they do play it is more as an accompaniment to the soloists than was the case in the opening movement.

Structure and Tonality	139 bars, this can be thought of as a ritornello form with some fugal elements as explained below.

Fugue – bb1-46 for the 4 soloists accompanied by the continuo.
- Exposition bb1-33.
  - b1 – Subject (F major) announced by the tromba which was silent for the 2nd movement. There is also an imitative 1st countersubject (CS1) announced at the same time by the continuo. These two themes are always heard together throughout.
  - b7 – Real Answer in the oboe, CS1 still in the continuo. Another countersubject (CS2) is played by the tromba.
  - b13 – a shorter third countersubject (CS3) is introduced by the oboe and imitated by the tromba 2 bars later.
  - b21 – Subject in the violin
  - b27 – Answer in the recorder
  - b33 – A fugal Episode for recorder, oboe, violin plus continuo
- Middle entry.
  - b41 – Subject (C major) restated by the tromba. The continuo falls silent in order to lend weight to the entry of the ripieno.

Ritornello – b47 onwards, the movement changes into a more typical concerto grosso format with alternate tutti and solo episode sections (interestingly, these ritornello episodes are based on the subject and countersubjects from the opening fugue, which gives the impression that they could be fugal Middle Entries!).
- b47 – Tutti, C major. A new tutti theme, derived from the fugue subject, is announced by the oboe, closely imitated by the tromba and violin.
- b53 – Episode (C major moving to D minor). Subject played by the violin, answered by the oboe.
- b72 – Tutti, D minor. The subject is now heard in the ripieno violone and continuo, which then move into a restatement of the Tutti theme imitated by the tromba and recorder.
- b85 – Episode, in which the soloists each present CS3 first heard in b13. Starting in D minor, each entry moves sequentially around the circle of 5ths towards B♭ major.
- b97 – Tutti, B♭ major. Featuring the Tutti theme in the tromba, closely imitated by the oboe, violone and continuo. The other accompanying parts enter in a stretto.
- b107 – Episode, B♭ major. The subject is played by the oboe and answered by the recorder (b113) as the music moves back towards the tonic.

	• b119 – Tutti, F major. Similar to that starting a b72, the subject is heard in the violone and continuo on the dominant of F major. This leads into the Tutti theme in recorder/oboe/violin. The subject is heard one last time in the tromba (b136) over a tonic pedal to bring the work to a close.
Melodic Development	Much of the thematic material is derived from the opening fugue subject, which in turn can be traced back to the main Ritornello theme from the 1st movement. This gives the 3rd movement, indeed the whole concerto, a sense of thematic unity. **Subject** bb 1-4:  Similarities to the 1st movement Ritornello theme: • Repeated dactylic rhythms mostly in conjunct movement. • Diatonic, based around the notes of the tonic triad (F, A, and especially C). • A direct quotation from the opening 5 notes of the 1st movement are present in this subject (in brackets above). • Decorated by trills. The subject also contains **two motifs** that Bach uses to build more themes later on in the movement: • The opening 3 quavers (F-C-C), leaping up a perfect 5th with a pair of repeated notes. • The lower auxiliary note figure (C-B♭-C) in b1². Examples: 2nd countersubject (CS2, b7 tromba).  • Starts with the 3 quavers but varies the repeated notes with an octave leap. 3rd countersubject (CS3, bb13-14 oboe).  • Starts with the octave leap from CS2, but now tied over the barline as a suspension, which resolves into the auxiliary note figure. Tutti theme (b47 oboe). 

	• This theme is syncopated, starting on the 2nd quaver of b47. • The upward leap is now a perfect 4th, and there is an extra repeated quaver. • The auxiliary note figure is now inverted (b48 G-A-G). • The two motifs then combine in a descending sequence. • The imitation starting on the last quaver of b47 (violin) alternates lower and upper auxiliary notes as a contrast to the oboe lead. Notice how the themes dissipate into semiquaver passage work to provide continuity into the next thematic statement, e.g., oboe bb7-16 plays the subject, then semiquaver figures into CS3 followed by more semiquaver figures.
Harmony	• Mostly diatonic with modulations to related keys confirmed by perfect cadences, e.g., V-I in dominant C major bb40-41, subdominant B♭ major bb106-107. • Imperfect cadences are used to keep the music moving by avoiding the finality of a perfect cadence, e.g., I-V in C major bb62-63, and again in D minor two bars later. • b136 – tonic pedal F reinforces the tonality at the end, resulting in an unusual plagal IVc-I final cadence bb138-139.
Rhythm	• 2/4 time, Allegro assai (very fast). • The continuo cello and violone parts move mostly in quavers and semiquavers which drives the music onwards with purpose. • The fugue subject features dactylic rhythmic patterns (i.e., long-short-short). • Syncopated crotchets (bb10-11 CS2, tromba). • Semiquaver passage work (e.g., bb93-105 solo violin).

Texture	• bb1-27 – fugal texture to begin with as each of the 4 soloists enters with the subject.
	• Ripieno strings are silent for the first 46 bars. The continuo drops out at b41 to add weight to the ripieno entry in b47.
	• Contrasting alternate full tutti and reduced soli/continuo textures from b47 onwards, e.g., tutti b47, soli/continuo b57, tutti b72, etc., typical of ritornello form.
	• bb72-78 – contains a variety of different textures:
	  ○ **Counterpoint** between violone/continuo, recorder and ripieno 1st violin
	  ○ Detached chords tromba, ripieno 2nd violin/viola
	  ○ **Inner dominant pedal** in tromba, sounding an A in the key of D minor
	• bb97-103 – tutti passage starts with **stretto** entries for all parts:
	  ○ Sustained ripieno violins
	  ○ Close imitation, one quaver apart (tromba lead, followed by oboe, violone and continuo)

	o Parallel motion: recorder/violin in 6ths, oboe and violone/ continuo in compound 3rds • bb136-139 – Final Subject/CS1 entry accompanied by homophonic detached chords.

Sample questions

In Section A of the examination there will be one question on each of the two prescribed works. You must choose to answer **one** of these **two** questions (as well as a third 'musical links' question which will be discussed later). Here are four sample questions based on the *Brandenburg Concerto no. 2* to use for practice. You may answer these in continuous prose or detailed bullet points, and you should allow around 30 minutes under timed conditions to complete each question. Reference should be made to an unmarked copy of the score and remember to give precise locations for the musical features you discuss.

1. *Brandenburg Concerto no. 2* is regarded as an example of how Bach's music represents the height of the Baroque style. Discuss **at least three** contrasting passages that illustrate this view.
2. Bach uses a wide range of instrumental timbres and textures in *Brandenburg Concerto no. 2*. Discuss and illustrate this view, making detailed references to the score.
3. Discuss Bach's use of structure and tonality in the **1st movement** of *Brandenburg Concerto no. 2*.
4. Discuss the changing relationship between the soloists' and ripieno parts across each of the three movements of *Brandenburg Concerto no. 2*. Refer in detail to specific passages of music.

DANCES OF GALÁNTA (1933) – ZOLTÁN KODÁLY

Introduction

This Prescribed Work was composed by Zoltán Kodály (1882–1967) for the 80th anniversary of the Budapest Philharmonic Society in his native Hungary. He took his inspiration from the small town of Galánta, which was part of the Kingdom of Hungary during his childhood there, but is now in present-day Slovakia. Kodály explained that his inspiration for the piece came in two parts:

> At that time there existed a famous [G]ypsy band that has since disappeared. This was the first 'orchestral' sonority that came to the ears of the child. The

forebears of these [G]ypsies were already known more than a hundred years ago. About 1800 some books of Hungarian dances were published in Vienna, one of which contained music 'after several Gypsies from Galánta'. They have preserved the old traditions. In order to keep it alive, the composer has taken his principal themes from these old publications.

Kodály chose several of these dances for his piece, with five of them making up the principal sections of the one-movement structure. He also wanted to recreate the *verbunkos* style of the aforementioned Gypsy band. *Verbunkos* was a Hungarian/Gypsy dance style with march-like accompaniments from the 18th century that was used to recruit young men into the army, with contrasting slow and fast sections, alternating swagger with foot-stomping energy and excitement.

Kodály's piece is much more than an arrangement of Gypsy folk tunes; they are infused and combined with an eclectic range of styles from 19th-century Romanticism to Impressionism, and even Atonality, to showcase these traditional melodies within a modern 20th-century Hungarian style of music.

Instrumentation

The piece is scored for orchestra, but not of the size often called for by 20th-century composers:

- Woodwind – 2 each of flute (2nd player also plays piccolo), oboe, clarinet, bassoon
- Brass – 4 french horns, 2 trumpets
- Percussion – timpani, triangle, campanelle (glockenspiel), tamburo piccolo (side drum)
- Strings (1st/2nd violins, violas, cellos, double basses)

Kodály gives the clarinet a prominent solo role, representing the *tárogató*, a single-reed instrument resembling a clarinet he probably first heard in the Galánta gypsy band. The cello section is also regularly given the melody, possibly because Kodály learned to play the cello in Galánta. As an ethnomusicologist and composer, Kodály was passionate about collecting local folk tunes and creating art music that was distinctively Hungarian. His colourful orchestrations sound similar to those of the Russian nationalist composers Rimsky-Korsakov and Mussorgsky, who were also working towards a similar goal for their own country.

Structure	**N.B.** – the Universal Edition score printed bar numbers are incorrect after bar 95; there is an extra uncounted bar between b95 and b100! This is simple enough to correct, but be aware that the numberings below are based on those in the score as it stands.
	
	One movement with 607 bars in total. There are five principal gypsy dances (as well as some additional ones) featured in this piece. Broadly speaking, the piece follows the form of a *verbunkos*, a traditional Hungarian style of dance and instrumental music comprising two sections; slow (*lassu*) with dotted rhythms, and fast (*friss*) with wild virtuosic running semiquaver passages.
	
	bb1-235 – slow (*lassu*)
	bb236-607 – fast (*friss*)
	
	However, within these broad sections lies a freer, more complex structure made up of sections and subsections, with recurring themes to unify the work as a whole:
	
	Introductio.n bb1-49 – a fantasia-like opening section.
	• Features the first of the folk melodies in this piece, and a series of 32nd note (demisemiquaver) flourishes. These 2 ideas alternate initially, and are then combined from b19.
	• The first melody is heard on various solo instruments, e.g., b1 cello section, b10 horn, b37 clarinet.
	• Clarinet cadenza b45 segues straight into…
	Ritornello section bb50-235 – featuring 3 of the principal Hungarian Gypsy dance melodies; the **1st Dance** acts like a recurring ritornello theme, with the **2nd** and **3rd Dances** heard as episodes.
	• bb50-93 – the passionate **1st Dance** is heard in the clarinet b50, then *ff* upper strings/woodwind b66, and cellos (with a shorter version) b82. Orchestral climax at b88 starts a link passage into the next section.
	• bb93-150 – **2nd Dance**, in binary form (AABB):
	    ○ A – a jauntier theme played by the flute b96, repeated with additional piccolo b103
	    ○ B – more forceful answering phrase is heard at b109 (1st violin/viola/clarinet), repeated by solo flute b113
	    ○ Short link passage b145 extending the B phrase
	• bb151-172 – a shorter reprise of the **1st Dance** in *ff* upper strings/woodwind. Link passage from b167.
	• bb173-228 – **3rd Dance**, again in binary form:
	    ○ A – 2 x 8-bar phrases bb173-188, solo oboe, then flute
	    ○ B – 2 more 8-bar phrases bb189-204, solo oboe, then piccolo
	    ○ Link passage where Kodály develops fragments of the B phrase, accelerating towards the next section

- bb229-235 – a brief reprise of the **1st Dance**, followed by a descending linking phrase for lower strings/woodwind

4th Dance bb236-333

- Featuring two phrases in the *friss* style; an exciting syncopated melody b236, and another with rapid semiquaver passages b268.
- Syncopated melody accelerates to a climax b334 leading straight into the next section.

Poco meno mosso bb334-420 – not quite as fast as the 4th Dance:

- 12-bar introduction establishing both the accompaniment and B♭ major tonality.
- bb346-377 – another binary form folk tune similar in character to that heard earlier from b96.
- bb378-420 – a link passage developing the theme and introducing hints of the next.

5th Dance bb421-607 – an even faster Finale section recalling several dances from earlier in the piece:

- b421 – a short ostinato-like phrase, viola and 2nd violin in canon.
- b443 – a phrase built from a 2-bar motif with a distinctive ♪♩♪ syncopated rhythm and semiquaver runs.
- b490 – a reprise of the **4th Dance** phrases (b236 and b268). As before the syncopated melody is used to build a climax bb525-542.
- b543 – **5th Dance** returns, building to a sudden pause and silence at b565.
- b566 – **Coda: 1st Dance** ritornello reappears in its original *Andante* tempo, passing from flute to oboe and clarinet, which plays another cadenza – a reminder of the **Introduction**.
- b579 – a final frantic reprise of the **5th Dance.**

Melody	Kodály took all of his thematic material from Gypsy dances specifically from Galánta, found in collections of Hungarian dances published in Vienna c.1800.
	
	Introduction theme bb1-5
	• Verbunkos style slow double-dotted rhythms with conjunct 32nd note auxiliary and passing note flourishes.
	• Dorian mode on A (ABCDEF#G); the opening F# makes the tonality uncertain to begin with.
	• Irregular 5-bar phrase.
	• Narrow range of a minor 7th typical of folk melodies.
	• Developments:
	   ○ b10 – transposed a 5th higher
	   ○ b19 – extended to 7 bars via a descending sequence
	   ○ bb222-231 – augmented 2nd C#-B♭ typical of the verbunkos style
	   ○ b37 – clarinet plays a chromatic variant which rises in sequence to a climax on high C (b43)

1st Dance bb50-65

- Kodály replaces the original straight semiquaver rhythms with a more elaborate verbunkos-style dotted pattern with the semiquavers compressed into triplet turn-like figures:

Original

Kodály

- Starts in E minor, ends in A minor.
- 16 bars, 2 × 8-bar mostly conjunct phrases in binary form:
  - 1st phrase is built from a 2-bar melody repeated in a descending sequence. Usually preceded by a rising glissando up to the first note. Cadences on repeated dominant B's with a prominent rising octave leap.
  - 2nd phrase has more quaver movement, especially the four sostenuto notes in b59.
- Several Lombardic/Scotch Snap rhythms, often accenting the 3rd beat, e.g., b503, 513.
- Developments:
  - b67 – theme is reharmonized and has a more chromatic ending bb78-79
  - b164 – the quavers of b79 are elaborated with repeated semiquavers
  - b229 – theme is heard in the Lydian Dominant scale on B♭ (B♭CDEFGA♭); the C#'s are chromatic auxiliary notes

2nd Dance bb96-118 – A♭ minor (originally in A minor), 2 phrases in AABB in Binary form, ends in D♭ major.

- 1st phrase: Kodály transposed the original melody down a semitone, and again converts straight semiquavers into dotted patterns (here the dots are often replaced by 32nd note rests). Irregular phrasing; 7 bars first time, 6 bars on repeat.
- 2nd phrase: largely unchanged except for an extension to the D♭ major ending using repeated broken triads. Another verbunkos-style augmented 2nd b111 (G♮- F♭).
- Developments:
  - b123 – 1st phrase heard in exotic sounding parallel 4ths
  - b134 – a 3-part triadic version of the 2nd phrase
  - b142 – the final D♭ broken triads now in 32nd notes and used in the following link passage

3rd Dance bb173-204 – D major, repeated 8-bar phrases in Binary form (AABB), 32 bars in total.

- Both phrases share a repeated 2-bar melody with a syncopated motif at the start followed by conjunct semiquavers and quavers.

- 1st phrase: diatonic, ends on the dominant (A).
- 2nd phrase: mostly diatonic apart from one chromatic lower auxiliary note (G# b192).
- Developments:
  - The first half of the 2nd phrase is transposed into G major b205 and the more distant E♭ major b213
  - Between these transpositions the second half of the 2nd phrase is abruptly pulled back into D major in a quicker Animato tempo. These udden tempo changes are another feature of Gypsy music, and were also used by Brahms in his Hungarian Dances

4th Dance bb236-275 – 2 contrasting Allegro phrases:
- 1st phrase bb236-247: 2 x 6-bar phrases in A minor, each featuring a chain of conjunct syncopated crotchets with a final semiquaver flourish in the 6th bar. One phrase ends on the dominant E, the other on the tonic A.
- Developments:
  - b252 – played in parallel 6ths (upper strings and woodwind)
  - b283 – used as a counterpoint to another theme in the violins
  - b315 – extended to 7 ½ bars
  - b322 – extended to 12 bars in diminished triads rising in parallel motion to a climax on G♭ b334
- 2nd phrase bb268-271: 2 x 2-bar question and answer phrases, mostly in semiquavers E major scales. One phrase ends on the dominant B, the other on the tonic E.
- Developments:
  - b272 – repeated an octave higher, modified to sound like the dominant of A minor (i.e., C♮ instead of C#)
  - b303 – repeated in B major (clarinet) and the dominant of A minor b311 (1st violin), alternating with the 1st (syncopated) phrase

Poco meno mosso bb346-377 – B♭ major, repeated 8-bar phrases in Binary form (AABB), 32 bars in total.
- 1st phrase: angular opening bar followed by conjunct movement in the next.
  - Alternate tonic and dominant (B♭/F) first notes in each bar
  - Decorated with appoggiaturas (b3462 E♮ rising to F) and turns (b3491)
  - Dotted rhythms and staccato/legato markings give the same jaunty feel heard in the 2nd Dance (b96 onwards)
- 2nd phrase: more conjunct than the 1st phrase.
  - b363 – syncopated falling octave F's: ♪♩ ♪ becomes an important motif in the 5th Dance

- o Switches between tonic minor (D♭'s bb362-365) and major (D♮'s bb366-369)
- o Decorated with turns (b365) and grace notes (b369)

5th Dance bb421-450 – 2 contrasting Allegro vivace phrases:
- 1st phrase: 4-bar ostinato melody mostly in quavers, centred on A minor.
  - o Quickly transposed to other tonal centres (E♭ b430 piccolo/oboe, D b433viola, B b438 trumpets)
- 2nd phrase bb443-450: an exhilarating 8-bar melody in A minor, built from two 1-bar figures:
  - o b443 – the syncopated falling octave motif heard in the Poco meno mosso (b363)
  - o b444 – mostly conjunct semiquaver runs
- Developments:
  - o b579 – syncopated octave D's are filled in with chromatic semiquavers
  - o b604 – syncopated octaves repeated 4 times by the whole orchestra in unison to end the piece.

Tonality and Harmony	A variety of tonalities can be heard in this piece from several times and places: **Introduction** • b1 – opening melody is in **Dorian mode on A.** • b6 – 32nd note arpeggios outline the **Gypsy Dorian scale** on A with its distinctive raised 4th (ABCD#EF#G). • b27 – in the key of A minor, with **19th-century Romantic** style chromatic chords and extensions:  Am G⁹⁽⁴⁻³ suspension⁾ F E⁷⁽⁴⁻³ suspension⁾ Dm⁷ dim⁷ᵗʰ Am⁷/C B⁷⁽♭⁵,⁹⁾ • bb37-40 – Impressionist style **chromatic non-functional** harmony: o | diminished 7th on A | C⁷/ B♭ | dim 7th (A) | French augmented 6th (B♭DEG#) | **1st Dance bb50** • Centred on E minor and moving to A minor, but the key is obscured by chromatic chords and the absence of conventional cadences, e.g., bb63-65: | Dm⁷, G⁷ | Aˢᵘˢ⁴ | A major (**tierce de Picardie**) |. • Extended chords, e.g., b66 dominant 9th on D, b68 G¹¹ (no 3rd). • Complete **circle of 5ths** in the bass underpinning the chromatic harmony, bb79-85.

- b88-92 – **pedal point** on G with alternate concords and discords.
- Perfect cadences are rare (bb81^2-82^1 V^{7}b^9-I in C major) and again avoided at the end of the section for continuity bb92-94:
  - | G | G/F | | Eb (which turns out to be V of Ab minor)

2nd Dance

- **Functional harmony** confirming Ab minor:
  - Dominant pedal bb93-99
  - bb100-102: | Augmented 6th (Fb) | Ic V^7 | I |

3rd Dance – D major

- **Folk style drone** on D and A roots most of this section in D major.
- Mostly **diatonic** chords.
- bb213-220 – sudden shift into Eb major abruptly cancelled by functional harmony in D, with a circle of 5ths and V^7-I perfect cadence.

4th Dance -

- Begins on A minor, but the tonal centre shifts with increasing frequency as the section progresses, e.g., b268 E major, b276 D minor, b299 B.
  b307 E.
- Inner dominant pedal E bb236-247.
- Bare sounding harmony in **parallel 4ths and 5ths** bb299 and 307.
- Folk style drone bass on E and B bb264-275.
- 20th-century **quintal harmony** (chords built on 5ths instead of 3rds) bb258-262.
- bb322-334 – rising chromatic diminished triads over an F pedal; dominant preparation for Bb major.

Poco meno mosso

- Bb major to start, confirmed by dominant inner pedal and ostinato tonic and dominant chords.
- bb362-369 – instead of following the harmony suggested by the Bb major melody, Kodály reharmonizes this in Db major before moving back towards the tonic. Again the expected perfect cadence bb368-369 is avoided with an interrupted cadence (F^7- Gb^7).
- 20th-century style **atonal** link passage bb405-420 with a tritone ostinato bass (C and Gb).

	5th Dance
	• bb443-450 – repeated functional II-V-I progression in A minor, although the leading note G# is not present, giving a modal effect. However, the final two bars have a more tonal sounding Ic-V-I perfect cadence in A minor.
	• The II-V-I outline can also be heard in related keys, e.g., C major bb451-456, E minor bb459-464.
	• bb502-505 – bare parallel 5ths.
	• bb566-578 – Impressionistic chromatic non-functional harmony over a descending bass recalling the opening of the piece:
	  ○ b566 G#m/D#
	  ○ b569 E⁷/D
	  ○ b571 C#m
	  ○ b573 augmented 6th on C♮ (C♮EGA#).
	• bb604-607 – final syncopated octave E's and A's outline an emphatic final perfect cadence.

Rhythm and Tempo	*Dances of Galánta* features a number of rhythm and tempo devices typically found in the verbunkos style and Hungarian/Gypsy dance music:
	• The tempo gradually speeds up over the course of the piece as a whole. Starting at *Lento* ♩ = 54, the tempo eventually reaches *Allegro vivace* ♩ = 152 at b421, and is even quicker from b579.
	• *Ritenuto* markings are used to emphasise expressive moments in the melody, e.g., on the quavers at b75.
	• *Stringendo* markings are used to create extra momentum and excitement, e.g., b326.
	• Sudden *animato* phrases interrupting the prevailing tempo, e.g., bb209 and 217.
	• The dances are in either 2/4 or 4/4 time.
	• Typical rhythms include:
	  ○ Double-dotted notes followed by 32nd note flourishes, e.g., bb1-4
	  ○ Lombardic or 'Scotch Snap' rhythms, e.g., the 3rd beats of bb50-52
	  ○ Syncopated figures followed by semiquaver runs, e.g., bb443-450
	  ○ March-like accompaniments with alternating on-beat bass notes and off-beat chords, e.g., 2nd Dance b93 onwards
	• Some 20th-century features are also present:
	  ○ Unusual time signatures, e.g., 1/4, b108
	  ○ Score is full of detailed markings for accents/staccato, e.g., 1st violin b443-450
	  ○ Impressionist style flexible tempi, pauses and 32nd note flourishes (Introduction bb1-49)

Texture	**Introduction**

Introduction
- bb1-18 – unaccompanied cello section solo, which then acts as a tonic pedal for the 32nd note flourishes in contrary motion (upper strings/flute). Rescored for solo horn b10, with cellos and piccolo joining in the answering flourishes.
- bb37-43 – clarinet solo accompanied by rapid 32nd note arpeggios in contrary motion and multi-stopped pizzicato strings. Tutti climax at b43.
- Clarinet cadenza bb45-49.

1st Dance
- Concerto style alternating solo and tutti sections:
  - b50 – solo clarinet with homophonic strings and french horns
  - b66 – tutti, with melody in flute, clarinet and upper strings plus sustained homophonic chords
  - b74 – solo for clarinet, 1st violins and cellos with a lighter chordal accompaniment
  - b82 – tutti, melody in lower strings and woodwind, with a slow march-like alternate bass/chords

2nd Dance
- b96 – solo flute with detached pizzicato string chords. Piccolo joins the flute melody and octave higher at b103.
- alternate tutti and solo sections.
- b129 – exotic rescoring of the melody on repeat:
  - Melody in parallel 4ths (flute/piccolo/2nd oboe)
  - Detached chords (pizzicato strings/muted trumpets)
  - Off-beat woodwind chords decorated with turns (1st oboe) and mordents (clarinets)
- b151 – reprise of the 1st Dance now with melody played *ff* across 3 octaves (upper strings/woodwind) with sustained chords (lower strings/woodwind/horns).

3rd Dance
- b197 – delicate high tessitura scoring:
  - Piccolo solo with clarinet countermelody
  - *Divisi* 1st violin harmonics, other strings play pizzicato
  - Glockenspiel and triangle outline the pulse and harmony
- bb205-216 – antiphony between woodwind and strings.

4th Dance
- Syncopated 1st phrase in **parallel motion** in various intervals: octaves (b236 strings), 6ths (b252 1st and 2nd violins), 4ths (b299 trumpets/2nd violins).
- b258 – syncopated phrase heard in close **canon**; off-beat piccolo/clarinets lead, followed by on-beat horn 1 bar later.

- Folk-style drone **ostinato** accompaniments, e.g., lower strings bb248-282.
- b283 – 2-part **counterpoint** between syncopated phrase (bassoon/viola/double bass) and a second theme (violins/cellos).
- b315 – both 1st and 2nd phrases from the 4th Dance heard together in counterpoint (woodwind semiquavers, and strings/horns in close canon as before)

Poco meno mosso
- b346 – clarinet solo, with **detached ostinato chords**. Bass notes decorated with *glissandi* (bassoon/lower strings).
- b354 – theme rescored for bassoon/cello, with **arpeggios** added above the ostinato chords.
- b370-385 – **imitation** of melody between upper strings and woodwind.

5th Dance
- b421-442 – 4-bar ostinato melody played in **canon** between viola and 2nd violin, and then repeated in other entries as the texture builds. Accompanied by a **countermelody** b425 (flute/1st violin), sustained notes (horns/trumpets) and ostinato bass (timpani/lower strings).
- Frequent changes of texture to balance out the repetitive nature of the melodies:
  - b443-450 – 1st violin melody doubled with fragments between the woodwind. Energetic semiquaver double-stopped string accompaniment.
  - Folk-style '**oom-pah**' bass/chord accompaniment (b451-466 lower strings/horns)
  - bb467-470 – melody in bassoon and lower strings, with tutti off-beat chords
  - bb471-474 – 2-part counterpoint between upper strings/woodwind, and trumpets/lower strings/woodwind
- bb566-572 – 1st Dance theme passed between solo flute/oboe/clarinet, with *pp* divisi tremolo 2nd violin/viola chords.
- bb602-607 – dramatic 2-bar silence followed by final heavily accented tutti octaves.

Sample questions

In Section A of the examination there will be one question on each of the two prescribed works. You must choose to answer **one** of these **two** questions (as well as a third 'musical links' question which will be discussed later). Here are four sample questions based on *Dances of Galánta* to use for practice. You may answer these in continuous prose or detailed bullet points, and you should allow around 30 minutes under timed conditions to complete each question. Reference should be made to an unmarked copy of the score and remember to give precise locations for the musical features you discuss.

1. Béla Bartók once wrote: "If I were to name the composer whose works are the most perfect embodiment of the Hungarian spirit, I would answer, Kodály." Discuss this statement with clear reference to **at least three** passages in *Dances of Galánta*.
2. Discuss Kodály's use of melody and tonality in *Dances of Galánta*.
3. *Dances of Galánta* draws upon musical elements from both traditional Hungarian and Western cultures. Identify and explain **two (or more)** elements that have roots in traditional Hungarian music and **two (or more)** elements that originate from Western music.
4. Discuss Kodály's approach to rhythm and texture in *Dances of Galánta*. Refer in detail to specific passages of music.

LINKS BETWEEN THE PRESCRIBED WORKS (HL ONLY)

Question 3 requires HL candidates to compare and contrast *Brandenburg Concerto no. 2* with *Dances of Galánta* with regard to one or two musical elements or concepts. This means you must write about similarities and differences in the use of, for example, melody and rhythm between the prescribed works, taking care to ensure your points are relevant to the elements or concepts asked in the question. For example, in a question about Instrumentation, while it is true to state that both works contain keyboard instruments, this is not a significant musical link; but a comparative discussion of *how keyboard instruments are used in each work* is creditworthy in the IB examination.

The following table is a list of some of the musical links between *Brandenburg Concerto no. 2* and *Dances of Galánta*, along with the locations of possible examples. They are grouped together in musical elements with a brief outline of each link; you will of course need to add your own more detailed explanations – a useful revision task.

Comparative links

Structure	Brandenburg Concerto no. 2	Dances of Galánta
Ritornello form, with shortened reprises of the main theme in different keys	1st movement, b1 (F major), b23 (C major), b56 (B♭ major)	1st Dance, b50 (E minor), b151 (A minor), b229 (Lydian Dominant scale on B♭)
Complex structures using multiple forms	3rd movement: fugue b1, ritornello b47	b1 fantasia, b50 ritornello, b173 binary form, over-arching verbunkos form (slow bb1-235, fast bb236-607)
Themes/motifs used to unify the work as a whole	F-F-E motif, 2nd movt bb3³-4¹ violin heard earlier in 1st movt bb63⁴-64¹ flute	1st Dance used as a ritornello theme, and reprised in the coda b567

Melody	Brandenburg Concerto no. 2	Dances of Galánta
Virtuoso solo parts	High tromba, 1st movt bb15-16	Clarinet cadenzas, bb44 and 573
Themes built from 2-bar phrases with repeats and variations	1st movt bb0⁴-8³, 2nd movt bb1³-3² and bb3³-5² (violin)	1st Dance bb50-65 (clarinet), 3rd Dance bb173-180 (oboe)
Decorated with ornaments and non-chord notes	2nd movt (violin): b3 trill and accented passing note (E), b4 suspension, b5 appoggiatura	Poco meno mosso: b349 turn (clarinet), b353 glissando (bassoon/cello), b369 grace notes (1st violin)
Longer notes in themes developed by filling them in with shorter notes	1st movt b86 violin: quavers of ritornello theme replaced with additional semiquavers	5th Dance (violins): syncopated motifs bb543 and 545 filled in with semiquavers in bb551 and 553
Diatonic melodies	1st movt ritornello theme bb0⁴-8³ F major	3rd Dance bb173-188 D major (oboe/flute)
Conjunct themes with a narrow range	3rd movt fugue subject bb1-6 tromba (1 octave)	2nd Dance bb96-108 flute (diminished 4th G♮ – C♭)
Dissonant melodic intervals	*2nd movt bb8³-9¹ flute (diminished 4th G♯ – C)*	2nd Dance b111 1st violin (augmented 2nd G♮ – F♭)

Harmony/Tonality	Brandenburg Concerto no. 2	Dances of Galánta
Perfect cadences used to confirm keys	1st movt b8 (Ic-V-I in F major)	2nd Dance bb101-102 (Ic-V-I in A♭ minor)
Use of Interrupted cadences to avoid the finality of a perfect cadence and keep the music moving forwards	2nd movt bb62-63 (V-VI in D minor)	3rd Dance bb211-212 (V-VI in D major)
Extended chords	1st movt b51: Dominant minor 9th formed from D^7 chord and E♭'s in the melody (flute/oboe)	1st Dance bb66-69: dominant 9th on D, followed by G^{11} (no 3rd)
Complete circle of 5ths outlined in the bass	2nd movt bb49-56, starting and ending on A	1st Dance bb79-85, starting and ending on E♭
Chromatic harmony	1st movt bb107-112: sequence of dominant 7ths, diminished 7th on B (b112)	Introduction bb37-40: diminished and dominant 7ths, augmented 6th on B♭ (b40)
Tierce de Picardie	2nd movt b65 D minor key, ends with D major chord	2nd Dance b112 A♭minor phrase ends with A♭major chord
Tonic pedal to confirm the key	3rd movement bb136-139 (F)	3rd Dance bb173-209 (D)

Texture	Brandenburg Concerto no. 2	Dances of Galánta
Alternate solo/tutti passages	1st movt bb9-23	5th Dance bb506-518
Polyphonic textures	3rd movt bb 1-46 fugal opening	4th Dance bb303-321
Melody in bass parts	1st movt bb56-57 part of the ritornello theme (cello and violone)	Poco meno mosso bb354-361 (bassoon and cello)
Canonic imitation	1st movt bb87^4 cello and violone, followed by tromba 2 beats later	4th Dance bb276 upper strings and woodwind, followed by trumpets 2 bars later

Texture	Brandenburg Concerto no. 2	Dances of Galánta
Parallel motion used to develop melodies	1st movt b93⁴ recorder and solo violin	2nd Dance bb123-133 woodwind instruments
Melody played in tutti octaves by whole orchestra	1st movt bb102⁴-104 ritornello theme	Coda bb604-607 syncopated motif
Melody passed between solo instruments	1st movt bb9-22 1st concertino theme (violin, oboe, recorder, tromba)	Coda bb567-572 reprise of the 1st Dance (flute, oboe, clarinet)
Homophonic melody and chordal accompaniment	3rd movt bb135-139	1st Dance bb50-93

Rhythm	Brandenburg Concerto no. 2	Dances of Galánta
Syncopated ♪♩ ♪ motifs	3rd movt b10 tromba	5th Dance b443 1st violin
Phrases linked together by semiquaver runs	3rd movt bb15-21 tromba	5th Dance bb447-451 1st violin

Contrasting

Feature	Brandenburg Concerto no. 2	Dances of Galánta
Tempo markings	Movements have fixed tempo markings; 1st movt has no tempo indication	Greater variety of tempo markings and changes of tempo, e.g., bb 561-579 (stringendo, andante maestoso, allegro molto vivace, etc.)
Tonality	Major/minor keys, with modulations to closely related keys	Diverse range of tonalities and modulations to distant keys: b6 Gypsy Dorian mode, b50 E minor, b93 A♭ minor, b405-420 Atonality
Harmony	Mostly functional with some chromatic passages using dominant and diminished 7ths	More harmonic variety; b93 functional harmony, b37 non-functional harmony, b173 drone, bb66-69 extended D^9 and G^{11} chords

Sample questions

In Section A of the examination there will be one compulsory question linking *Brandenburg Concerto no. 2* with *Dances of Galánta*. Here are three to use for practice. You may answer these in continuous prose or detailed bullet points and you should allow around 30 minutes to complete each question. Reference should be made to unmarked copies of both scores, and remember to give precise locations and explanations for the musical features you discuss.

1. Compare and contrast the use of harmony and tonality of each of the prescribed works, highlighting any significant musical links.
2. In what ways can both of the prescribed works be regarded as similar in their use of melody and melodic development?
3. Investigate significant musical links between the two prescribed works by comparing and contrasting their use of form and structure.

Section B

PERCEPTION AND ANALYSIS OF MUSICAL STYLES

This chapter will give you an overview of the typical musical features of each style that is often featured in this part of the examination. It is not possible to cover every eventuality here – there has been a vast amount of music created across world history – but it is possible to learn and revise the most important styles and the terminology associated with them. The IBO breaks these styles down into three main areas: Western Classical Music, Jazz and Pop, and World Music. Remember that for this examination Western Classical Music spans a period running from 1550 up to the present day – not just the style that emerged in Vienna at the end of the 18th century. The dates that are used for the different periods of Classical Music are not absolute; the Baroque period did not start the day after the Renaissance period ended! It is best to think of musical styles and periods as overlapping, constantly evolving and developing over time, with the dates given to indicate when certain methods and approaches to creating music were in vogue.

WESTERN CLASSICAL MUSIC

Renaissance Period (1550–1600)

Key features:

* Most Renaissance music was written for voices, either for church services and ceremonies (sacred), or for secular (i.e., non-church) purposes, such as private entertainment or dancing.
* Melodies are based on **modes**, but composers gradually added more accidentals. This is the start of the evolution towards major and minor keys established in the Baroque period. Most melodic movement is **conjunct** (step-wise); where there is a leap, it is almost always followed by a step back in the opposite direction.
* Textures tend to be **polyphonic**, with melodic lines **imitating** and weaving around each other. However, you will also hear some **homophonic**

phrases. Composers also liked to have passages where one group sang or played, followed by an answering phrase from another group. This is called **antiphony** and should not be confused with 'call and response', a term used to describe similar passages in African drumming or Blues.

- Harmony consists mainly of **root-position** and **first-inversion** chords, and composers also used **cadences** to round off sections or end pieces. As well as **perfect** (V–I) cadences, expect to hear **plagal** (IV–I, or 'Amen') and **imperfect** cadences, which always end on chord V. Sometimes a piece in a minor mode will end on a major chord – this is known as a **tierce de Picardie**.
- Other popular harmonic devices were the result of melodic lines interacting with each other. The most common example of this is the **suspension**, but another very distinctive effect was the **false relation**.
- Many Renaissance works are through-composed. This means they are based on a succession of ideas (points) which, in sacred music, were often discussed polyphonically – hence, the term 'counter-point'. Other important structures were Variations in keyboard works, binary forms in dances and strophic form in lute songs.

Genres, contexts and composers

Church music to begin with was sung in Latin and intended to be sung *a cappella* (unaccompanied), and consisted mainly of **masses** and **motets**. The mass was a setting of parts of the rite of Holy Communion to music, and motets were based upon a few verses from the Bible and sung during the service or on special days in the Church year. But the Reformation, in the dual form of the Church of England and the Catholic Council of Trent, had an influence on music for worship in two significant ways. Firstly, it was decreed that the words should be more easily heard, which meant an increase in the use of homophonic textures and solo voices at the expense of polyphony. This was a musical trend that continued into the early Baroque period. Secondly the Elizabethan regime demanded new sacred music to be written in English, so that everyone could understand the words. This gave rise to new genres, such as the **anthem**, like a motet but sung in English and sometimes accompanied by the organ. In the examination you may be able to tell which language is being sung, and the mass movements all begin with the same key words (*Kyrie, Gloria, Credo, Sanctus, Benedictus* and *Agnus*) so it is worth remembering them, as they will enable you to identify the genre accurately. Possible composers include Palestrina (Italy) and Byrd and Tallis (both England).

In Venice, the sacred music performed at St. Mark's Cathedral made great use of its architecture. There were two choir galleries, each with an organ built high into the opposing walls of the church. Giovanni Gabrieli, probably the finest composer of **polychoral** music, often wrote for three or more groups using combinations of voices and ceremonial instruments such as trombones and cornetts (a wooden trumpet with a brass mouthpiece).

The most important secular vocal genres were the **madrigal** and the **lute song (ayre)**. Madrigals originated in Italy and were written for a varied number of voice parts, usually with one singer on each part. They were mostly unaccompanied, and the texts were poems about love or were satirical, and were a popular form of self-entertainment in royal and aristocratic circles. Madrigals became a genre in which composers such as Monteverdi and Gesualdo felt they could freely experiment with new rhythm, melody and especially harmony, in their efforts to fully express the meaning of the text. Some of their music was controversial because of the strong dissonances they used, something which led Monteverdi to suggest there should be two separate ways of writing music; one for the Church (*prima prattica*) and another for secular society (*seconda prattica*). Their popularity spread to Elizabethan England where Byrd, Weelkes and Morley also used vivid word-painting to illustrate their poems. Ayres were often strophic in form and were usually performed by a solo voice with the lute accompanying; the most famous Renaissance musician across the courts of Europe in this genre was the English lutenist and composer, John Dowland.

In the Renaissance, instruments were secondary to voices, and they were mainly used for ceremony, dances and accompanying vocal music. Many instrumental pieces were simply transcribed from vocal pieces, but some original works were created. Variations were composed for a harpsichord-like instrument called the virginal, and dances were written for consorts (groups) of viols (a family of bowed string instruments) or crumhorns (double-reeded woodwinds like an oboe). A popular pair of dances was the **pavane and galliard**: the pavane was a stately dance in 2, while its partner was a livelier dance in 3. Like most dance music they had repeated sections, a constant tempo and periodic phrasing.

Baroque (1600–1750)

Key features:

- To begin with, textures were thinner and more homophonic (melody and chords). This was known as **monody**. However, polyphonic textures came back as the period went on.
- The **continuo** was the foundation for most genres of Baroque music; this consisted of a bass part (mostly cello but sometimes bassoon), and a

keyboard part (harpsichord or organ) improvised chords from figures written below the bass part – hence, the term **figured bass**. This is probably the most recognizable feature of Baroque music.

- Above the continuo parts, melodies were often written in long, winding phrases decorated with **ornaments,** such as trills, mordents and turns.
- Baroque pieces often only have one **affection** (mood) running from beginning to end. Contrast in the music was achieved by pitting a few instruments against many, or by alternating loud and soft sections (**terraced dynamics**) – note that *crescendo* and *diminuendo* were rarely used.
- Viols were gradually replaced by the violin family. This was the era of the great violin makers of Italy, such as Stradivarius. The violin, viola, cello and double bass formed the first complete section of the orchestra as we know it today. Woodwind (flute, oboe and bassoon), trumpets and timpani (kettle drums) were sometimes added to the strings and continuo.
- By around 1700 the Greek modes used in the Renaissance were reduced from seven to just two – Ionian and Aeolian, or major and minor. The French composer Rameau produced the first book about harmony and tonality, and J. S. Bach wrote his 48 Preludes and Fugues, two of each in every possible major and minor key.
- Several new structures evolved alongside **binary** (AB) form: **ternary** (ABA, especially in *da capo* aria), **rondo** (ABACA), **ritornello** (used frequently by Vivaldi in his concertos), and **fugue**, a type of piece using polyphonic texture.

Genres, contexts and composers

The Baroque period in music took its name from the ornate style of architecture that was in fashion. It was a time of experimentation, and many new musical genres were developed. It is customary to divide the 150-year period into three blocks of 50:

1600–50	Early Baroque (Monteverdi, Schutz)
1650–1700	Mid-baroque (Corelli, A. Scarlatti, Lully, Purcell)
1700–50	Late (or High) Baroque (Bach, Handel, Vivaldi)

You should try to familiarize yourself with the sound of each sub-period, as this will help you to date the music you hear more precisely.

The late Renaissance concept of seconda prattica, where the words were more important than the music, gave rise to monody, a solo voice with simple continuo accompaniment. The rhythms were composed to match as closely as possible the natural accents of speech, and melodies were designed to empha-size the meaning of the words (or 'word painting') with dramatic leaps and chromatic dissonances. This style of singing was called **recitative**, which became the most important way of conveying dialogue and storytelling in **opera**. The first operas in the early 1600s were based on ancient Greek stories and tragedies and consisted of little else but recitative, but Monteverdi soon realized the genre needed more variety and added short choruses and instru-mental pieces. Towards the end of the 17th century composers coupled their recitatives with **arias**, a more poetic, songlike piece in which characters could reflect or expand upon their situations as suggested by the preceding recitative.

Opera spread as a popular theatrical entertainment from Italy to France and England. Lully's operas for the court of King Louis XIV at Versailles fea-tured dances and what became known as the French Overture, an orchestral introduction to the opera with a slow section full of dotted rhythms followed by a fast section often with a fugal opening with the parts entering at differ-ent points with the same (or modified) theme. Henry Purcell's *Dido and Aeneas* featured French and Italian influences, as well as some distinctively English features, such as the use of Ground Bass in some arias. At the end of the 17th century Alessandro Scarlatti was developing the *da capo* aria and the Italian Overture. The *da capo* aria was cast in ternary form but written in binary (AB) with an instruction to repeat the first section, and the Italian Overture had three sections (fast–slow–fast) and would later go on to form the basis of the Classical Symphony. At the end of the Baroque period Handel was the best-known opera composer, and many of his works were premiered in London.

The Church still had a significant influence on society at this time, to the extent that opera was not permitted in theatres during holy seasons such as Lent. Instead, they put on **oratorios**, which re-told Bible stories without staging or costume, but in musical terms they are difficult to distinguish from opera – both contain overtures, recitative and aria, and choruses. The greatest oratorios of the Baroque period were composed by Bach and Handel, thus it is most likely that you will hear the words being sung in German or English. Bach was also well known for his **cantatas** (a form of miniature oratorio), which he wrote for the services at his churches in Leipzig, Germany.

During the Baroque period instrumental music gained more importance. A popular new genre was the **trio sonata**; 'trio' was a reference to the number of parts in the score, two melody lines and a figured bass part. But remember that continuo involves two players, a bass and a keyboard instrument, which actually makes a total of four players. There were two different types of trio sonata: **sonata da camera** (to be played in a room at home) and **sonata da chiesa** (for use in church), but they are both essentially **suites** of dances. These dance movements were almost always in the same key, cast in a Binary form that depended on the same tonal structure, with the A section moving from tonic to dominant, and the B section wending its way back to the tonic via a series of related keys. The best-known composers of trio sonatas were Corelli, Couperin, Bach and Handel. Although the number of movements could vary, there were four dances that were usually present in trio sonatas:

- Allemande – a German dance in 4/4 time and a moderate tempo.
- Courante (running) – a French dance in 3/2 or 6/4 and a fairly fast tempo.
- Sarabande – a slow stately dance from Spain in 3/4, with an accent on the second beat.
- Gigue (Jig) – a fast French/English dance in a compound time such as 6/8.

Another important new genre was the **concerto**, either in the form of a **concerto grosso** (for a group of soloists, orchestra and continuo) or a solo concerto. The idea of contrasting groups in Baroque orchestral music can be traced back to the antiphonal pieces of Giovanni Gabrieli at St Mark's, Venice. Corelli, Bach and Handel are again notable composers in this genre, but the most important composer here is Vivaldi, with his distinctive driving rhythms and flowing melodic lines. Vivaldi taught violin at an orphanage for girls in Venice and most of his concertos were written for recitals by the orchestra he formed there. In a concerto grosso the solo group – typically two violins and a cello – was called the **concertino**, and the main body of strings and continuo (around twenty in number) was known as the **ripieno**. Many concertos had three movements (fast–slow–fast), and a popular structure for the fast movements was the **ritornello**, literally meaning 'return', because the main **tutti** theme (played by all) would reappear at regular intervals in related keys. In between these *ritornellos* there would be contrasting solo sections for the concertino or single soloist, accompanied by the continuo.

   Fugue can be regarded as both a genre and a texture. It is a polyphonic piece based on one main theme (the **subject**), which is then imitated between the different parts (voices). At the start of a fugue the voices enter one by one using the subject. When all have entered, the opening section (**exposition**) has concluded. What follows is a series of episodes (freer material sometimes derived from the subject) and **middle entries** of the subject in related keys. The fugue ends with the final entries in the tonic key. Fugues can be vocal or instrumental and can appear in all of the other genres mentioned previously, either as a self-contained movement, or as part of a larger movement, in which case it is known as a **fugato**. All the mid- and late-Baroque composers wrote fugues, but the outstanding composer here is J. S. Bach, who wrote many for harpsichord and organ in particular, and he would often pair them with a prelude (literally an introductory piece) or a toccata (a piece featuring rapid and skilful finger work). **Tip:** when you hear a fugue, try to listen for the order in which the voices or parts enter.

Classical (1750–1810)

Not to be confused with 'Classical' in the record shop sense, where it is used to refer to music across all the style periods discussed here. This period features the music of Haydn, Mozart and the early works of Beethoven.

Key features:

- A far greater use of **homophonic textures** than the Baroque. **Melody and chords** is very common, and pieces were lighter and clearer than the weightier polyphonic sound of the Late Baroque. However, polyphonic textures do still exist in this period, so do not assume too much!
- Classical music sounds **elegant**, **polished**, and **well-balanced** in both its phrasing and structure. As in all music there is expression and emotion, but here it is always kept in check by its structure.
- Within the bounds of the structure, Classical pieces had a **wider range of contrast and variety**. Composers would write different sections of their music in different moods by contrasting the keys, themes, rhythms and dynamics.
- Melodies are usually **shorter** than their spun-out Baroque counterparts and have clear **question and answer phrases** marked by **cadences**.
- Harmonies are still **diatonic**, but some chromatic chords are creeping in, such as **diminished 7ths** and **augmented 6ths**. Devices such as **pedal points** become more common.
- Dynamics had now developed into a more dramatic set of instructions, such as **crescendo/diminuendo** and **sforzando**.
- The harpsichord continuo filling in the chords for the Baroque orchestra was made obsolete by the development of the Classical orchestra's **woodwind section** (2 each of flutes, oboes, clarinets and bassoons).
- The harpsichord was also no match for the **piano**, with its ability to play at different dynamics. A very typical piano texture to listen out for was **Alberti Bass**, a type of broken chord accompaniment.
- New forms of instrumental music evolved, many with a sonata-like multi-movement format, e.g., **symphony**, **string quartet**, **sonata**, **concerto**.
- **Sonata Form** is the most significant new structure. Not the form of a *whole* sonata but a *single movement within* that sonata! Remember – **exposition** (themes presented in contrasting keys), **development** (themes developed/ explored/combined in several keys), **recapitulation** (all themes restated in home/tonic key only).

Genres, contexts and composers

Some significant changes were afoot during the Classical period. For the first time, all the significant composers were based in one part of Europe, namely Austria and Germany. For a time, these composers were all based in the city of Vienna, and this marks the start of what can be seen as a domination of Western music by this region. Instrumental music was for the first time more important than music for voices. Although the **piano** became fashionable in the second half of the 18th century, it had been invented at the end of the 17th century. Unlike the harpsichord's keys, which were plucked, the piano's keys were struck by hammers, and the amount of force and touch used on each key could be varied to create dynamic contrasts, smooth **legato** or detached **staccato** styles of playing. Many piano sonatas were written by Haydn, Mozart and Beethoven, mostly for entertaining small audiences in aristocratic households, but other purposes gradually evolved: some were written for playing for pleasure at home, while some of Beethoven's later works are on a grand scale more appropriate to the concert hall as the pianos became larger and more powerful in design. Indeed, it was not only the aristocracy who would listen to live music – the emerging **middle class** had disposable income which they could spend on attending concerts, opera and even their own instruments. This in turn changed the very nature of the composer's employment; Haydn was one of the last composers to hold a court position, and Beethoven was the first truly freelance composer writing music commissioned by a variety of patrons. Many of Beethoven's symphonies and concertos were premiered at subscription concerts. Furthermore, with more people owning and playing instruments, a new market arose for music that was playable in the home: music for piano, voice and small chamber ensembles.

The **symphony** can be thought of as a 'sonata for orchestra' and it grew out of the Baroque Italian overture because is was usually in three sections (fast–slow–fast), which became separate movements. Haydn is usually credited with adding a Minuet and Trio after the slow movement to complete the familiar four-movement format we know today:

1st movement – Allegro (fast) in tempo, sometimes preceded by a slow Introduction – usually in Sonata Form.
2nd movement – Adagio (slow), often more lyrical – structure can be ABA (Ternary), Theme and Variations, or Sonata Form.
3rd movement – Minuet and Trio (fairly fast, 3/4 time) – a dance movement that Beethoven later changed to the faster Scherzo.
4th movement – Allegro, usually light and joyful in mood – structure can be a Rondo (ABACA), Sonata Form again, or a hybrid Sonata-Rondo

(ABA–C–ABA – the two ABA's are equivalent to the Exposition/Recapitulation and the C is the 'Development' section).

It is worth learning these designs, as it will enable you to discuss the wider structure and context of the fairly short CD extract you may be given. Other genres, such as Trios and String Quartets, also had four movements in this layout. Sonatas and Concertos often only had three of these movements, with the Minuet omitted.

The Classical **Concerto** is a continuation of the Baroque solo concerto with two new features: the double exposition and the cadenza. The **double exposition** is a modification made to the first movement's sonata form structure; the orchestra and soloist each have their own exposition – the orchestra play first, followed by the soloist accompanied by the orchestra. After this the development and recapitulation follow as usual, but near the end of the recapitulation, the orchestra pauses on a Ic (tonic 2nd inversion) chord. The soloist plays the **cadenza**, a virtuoso passage based on the main themes where s/he can display their technical brilliance. The prearranged signal for the end of the cadenza is a trill, at which the orchestra come in again to round off the movement with a coda. Cadenzas are often improvised but some composers preferred to write their own.

A large amount of chamber music was written mainly for home entertainment, and it is worth noting a couple of points here. Firstly, whereas the Baroque trio sonata actually required four players, from the Classical period onward the ensemble name equals the numbers of players. By the end of the period Beethoven had composed a Septet (seven players), and the early Romantic composer Schubert an Octet (eight); both sound like small-scale orchestral works, but are still capable of an intimate sound. The **string quartet** came to be regarded as the perfect chamber music combination (2 violins, a viola and a cello), and Haydn was credited with creating the musical template followed by later composers. A feature of quartets to watch out for is the frequent changes in texture as a means of maintaining musical interest.

Classical works also started to become known by their nicknames, usually describing something heard in the piece. Haydn's symphony No. 94 was called 'The Surprise' because of the sudden fortissimo chords in the quiet second movement, and Mozart's string quartet K.465 was known as 'Dissonance' because of the remarkably chromatic introduction to the first movement.

Opera in the late Baroque period had reached a point where the singers held too much creative control; music was written for them to show off their vocal skills at the expense of the action and the storytelling. In the 1760s Gluck composed operas that redressed this imbalance with music that fitted and reflected the action, and more continuity from recitative to aria often merging the two. The finest operas written in this period are all by Mozart (*The Marriage of Figaro, Don Giovanni, The Magic Flute*). Mozart's operas took the genre to a new level, with music written to match every subtle change in the drama or the characters, not just for the singers but for the orchestra as well.

Beethoven (1770–1827)

You will notice from Beethoven's dates that they fall across both the Classical and Romantic periods – and this is also true of his music. As mentioned earlier he was the first freelance composer and inspired the Romantic composers after him. It is usual to divide up his music into three periods:

First period – similar in style to Haydn and Mozart (Beethoven had some lessons with Haydn in Vienna). Symphonies 1 and 2, string quartets 1–6, piano sonatas 1–12 (there are 32 in all).

Second period – Classical forms modified and expanded. Music is on a much grander scale and has more impact, drama and conflict. Orchestra becomes larger and includes piccolo, double bassoon and trombones. Symphonies 3–8, 'Razumovsky' quartets, the 'Moonlight' sonata comes from this period. Beethoven's deafness was on the increase.

Third period – these works were composed entirely in his aural imagination; he was by now totally deaf. The 9th Symphony (the first ever to feature voices and bass drum, cymbals and triangle), the late quartets and piano sonatas.

Romantic (1810–1900)

Although all composers look to express themselves through their music, the Classical style balanced this out with the importance attached to structure and form. In the 19th century, however, this balance was clearly shifted towards expressiveness.

Key features:

- **Lyrical melodies**, often using more chromaticism. Key changes became more distant from the Tonic; earlier periods modulated to the dominant and relative minor, but mediant, or third-related key changes (e.g., from B major to G major) were popular in the Romantic period.
- Harmony also became more **chromatic**, with **extended chords** (9ths, 11ths and even 13ths) and strong **dissonances**. All of which started to undermine the tonal system established in Baroque times.
- Following Beethoven's lead, the Romantic orchestra was much larger than before. A fully fledged **brass section** became possible with the introduction

of **valves**. More strings and woodwind were often needed to match the power of the brass.

- Huge diversity in the range of different genres; from short 2-minute songs and piano miniatures up to 4-hour operas.
- Closer links to art and literature lead to the development of **programme music** inspired by fantastic and imaginative stories, poems and paintings. Classical forms were modified and altered to fit with the programme, and **recurring themes** were used to hold the large-scale pieces together.
- Great increase in technical skills and **virtuosity**, particularly in piano and violin. Some Romantic pieces were considered unplayable when they were first published!

Genres, contexts and composers

The German **Lied** was a song written for solo voice and piano – not just an accompaniment here, but an equal partnership. The piano often cleverly created the mood and drama of the poem with its own preludes, interludes and postludes. Most Lieder were either strophic (same music for each verse) or through-composed (different music for each verse). The best known composer here is Schubert, who wrote over 600 Lieder, including 9 in one day. They range from the dramatic chase of *Erlkonig* (The Erlking) to the lost love of *Ihr Bild* (Her Portrait). Sometimes songs were grouped together in 'song-cycles' with a theme or story behind them. Schumann and Brahms were also notable Lieder composers.

Piano music evolved rapidly during the 19th century thanks to advances in the instrument's design and the abilities of the players. An iron frame was introduced, allowing greater tension on the wires, giving a wider dynamic and tonal range, further enhanced by the soft pedal. Chopin and Liszt exploited these advances to the full, writing preludes, stirring waltzes and serene nocturnes (literally 'night music'). Chopin was known for the influences of his native Poland (e.g., mazurkas) and his melodic **arabesques**, Liszt for his astounding virtuosity (e.g., *Grand Galop Chromatique*) but also moments of reflective beauty. Again, Schumann and Brahms are counted among the greatest of the Romantic pianists. Many middle-class households owned a piano, and a wide variety of music that could be played for personal pleasure was published.

Programme music (i.e., music that tells a story or paints a picture) was a very important feature of Romantic orchestral music written for the concert hall, and composers made full use of the new forces at their disposal. Many one-movement works, called either concert overtures or tone poems, were created. Mendelssohn's *Fingal's Cave* is an overture that evokes the wild coasts of Scotland, while Richard Strauss's *Till Eulenspiegel* tells through music the medieval tale of a practical joker and trickster who is eventually hanged for his crimes. On an even bigger scale, the 5-movement *Symphonie Fantastique* by Berlioz takes the listener through several different dreams the protagonist has about his beloved: a waltz at a ball, and the 'March to the Scaffold', where he is beheaded for a crime of passion, to name but two. In the examination you will only be played a short extract from these large-scale pieces, but there are good marks for structure and context to be scored if you can display some wider knowledge beyond what you can hear. For example, most programme music relies upon a recurring, or motto, theme to inform the listener of what is happening. This theme is then transformed and developed as the piece progresses in ways that accurately fit the drama or imagery with, for example, new rhythms or ornamentation.

The rapid rise in the technical virtuosity of solo performers led to an increase in the difficulty composers put into their concertos. Some of these were initially regarded as being impossible to play (e.g., Tchaikovsky's *Violin Concerto*). Many composers also regained creative control of the cadenza by writing their own instead of leaving it up to the soloist. As with other orchestral genres, there were experiments with the structure of movements, perhaps linking them together, or merging the movements into one continuous piece.

The two main countries for Romantic opera were Italy and Germany. Once again there was a trend away from separate numbers towards a more continuous music, integrating recitative and aria, sometimes lasting across a whole act. Giuseppe Verdi is considered one of the greatest opera composers; his characterisations were subtle and expressive, and the drama he created through his music was both direct and intense. Among the most popular of his operas is *Aida*, set in Ancient Egypt. Richard Wagner took the idea of integration to an extreme with his **music-dramas**. He preferred this term instead of 'opera', as he aimed to produce music for the stage which involved all of the arts. A very large orchestra played a significant role in Wagner's music-dramas, but its size and power posed a major problem for the singers. To enable them to be heard more clearly Wagner had a theatre specially built at Bayreuth, Germany, with the orchestra housed in a large pit below stage level. Among his finest achievements was the *Ring Cycle*, a series of four operas based on the legends of the Norse gods. Each of these operas were 3–4 hours long, and in order to keep the audience informed of the action Wagner devised a system of **Leitmotifs**, giving each character, object or place a unique theme. These melodies were woven into the music to show, for example, when a character was on stage or being referred to, and the melodies were modified to reflect the situation or mood.

During the 19th century, a group of composers sought to break away from the dominant German musical influences of the period by using the folk melodies and dance rhythms from their own countries in their compositions. This movement became known as **Nationalism**. The first nationalist composers came from Russia and were known as the 'Mighty Handful' after their powerful orchestral works. Of these, the best known are Mussorgsky (*Pictures at an Exhibition*) and Rimsky-Korsakov (*Scheherazade*). In Bohemia (present day Slovakia and the Czech Republic), Dvorak's *Slavonic Dances* used the local dances, such as the polka and furiant, while Smetana's *Vltava* is a tone poem that traces the course of the River Vltava (the Moldau) all the way to Prague. Other countries with nationalist composers were Norway (Grieg), Finland (Sibelius) and England (Vaughan Williams). Sibelius and Vaughan Williams, along with the Russian Shostakovich and the Hungarian Bartók ensured the nationalist movement continued well in to the 20th century.

Modern (1900–present)

Up until 1900 the periods of music history could be regarded as having one style, which was largely common to all of its composers. But the Modern period has seen an ever-increasing and exciting diversity of different styles, influences and experiments. Some common musical trends will be mentioned first, but thereafter it is easier to treat 20th-century music one style at a time.

Key features:

- The dominance of major–minor tonality was broken by **atonality**, a new system that treated all the notes of the chromatic scale as equals, with no sense of tonic and dominant. Other tonal systems evolved, such as the **whole tone scale**, and older systems such as modes were revived.
- Melodies were more likely to be disjunct rather than conjunct, sometimes with extremely dissonant wide leaps.
- Harmonies were no longer subject to tonal relationships, so they became more dissonant and were also used purely for their effect.
- A more vibrant and energetic use of rhythm, with cross-rhythms, polyrhythms, odd time signatures, sudden changes of metre and accent.
- The changes of approach to rhythm were coupled with both the expansion of the percussion section in the orchestra and an increasing use of ethnic percussion instruments.
- A never-ending search for new timbres. Composers looked to use traditional instruments and voices in new and unusual ways, or use newly invented instruments; and with the advent of sound recording and synthesis, it became possible to shape and create sound as never before.

Impressionism

A style with links to the visual art of painters such as Monet, musical impressionism was first created by the French composer **Claude Debussy**. Like many forward-thinking composers, he was looking for a new direction away from the excesses of late Romanticism. In the same way that Monet blurred the outlines of his pictures, Debussy blurred the outlines of his music by avoiding the use of conventional scales, chords and cadences. Instead, he wrote melodies that used modes and whole-tone scales, his triads were sometimes built on fourths rather than thirds (this is called **quartal harmony**), and he would often move 7th and 9th chords up and down in parallel motion. Debussy's orchestral pieces were full of new combinations of instrumental sound and texture, unusual rhythmic groupings and detailed tempo, phrasing and dynamics to achieve the subtle light and shade he wanted. Listen to *L'Apres-midi d'un faune* (1894) or the piano *Preludes* to get a feel for this unique musical style.

Arnold Schoenberg (1874–1951)

As with Monteverdi and Beethoven before, Schoenberg is a composer who stands between two style periods. He began his career as a Romantic composer writing music that was both highly polyphonic and harmonically complex. Schoenberg began to realize that he had reached the end of what he could say within the tonal system, and although other composers were moving toward the same position, he was the first to break ranks and produce the first atonal music. The dissonant sound of this music is challenging to listen to even now, but back in the early 20th century, Schoenberg risked controversy and alienation with this new direction. This new style was called **Expressionism**, because it sought to express darker emotions, such as fear.

The first atonal pieces (e.g., *Six Little Pieces* for piano, 1911) were short, sometimes only a few bars long. One of the main problems with discarding the tonal system was that suddenly the means by which longer pieces were structured was gone.

Schoenberg had to develop a new way of organising his music to give it more length and unity, and he devised a system he called the **Twelve-note system**, also known as **Serialism**. The twelve notes of the chromatic scale are first arranged in any order of the composer's choosing (the **prime order** or **tone row**). Melodies and harmonies can be created from the tone row as long as the notes in the row are used in strict order. More variety is achieved through developing the tone row by **transposing** it, or using it in **retrograde** (backwards), **inversion** (upside down), or **retrograde inversion** (a combination of both). Another technique Schoenberg invented was **sprechgesang**, a vocal style combining both singing and speech, which he used in *Pierrot Lunaire* (*Moonstruck Pierrot*), for soprano accompanied by five instruments. Two of Schoenberg's pupils, Webern and Berg, adopted his methods, and the three of them became known collectively as the **Second Viennese School**.

Neoclassicism

Some composers reacted against Romanticism by taking their inspiration from the music of the Baroque and Classical periods, when melody, structure and texture had more clarity. Many older structures and genres were rediscovered, such as concerto grosso and fugue. Neoclassical music can sometimes be hard to distinguish from the older styles it is based upon, because much of the melodic and harmonic language uses tonality. The differences often lie in the instrumentation, some abrupt changes of key, or chords are often coloured with added notes and dissonances, and a rhythmic approach that belongs more in the 20th century than the 18th. Neoclassical composers include Prokofiev (*Classical Symphony*), Stravinsky (*Pulcinella Suite*, based on music by the Baroque composer Pergolesi) and Shostakovich (*24 Preludes and Fugues* for piano, inspired by those of J. S. Bach).

Minimalism

This is a style based upon very small rhythmic and melodic motifs that are heavily repeated and gradually evolve and develop as the music progresses. Minimalism has its roots in the hypnotic beats of African drumming, with frequent syncopations, polyrhythms (different metres being played simultaneously) and layering of percussive textures. The American composer, Steve Reich, (born 1936) is the pioneer of Minimal music, and he has used many different media to create his works: *Clapping Music*, for two musicians to play anywhere; *Come Out*, composed with tape loops; and *New York Counterpoint*, for solo clarinet accompanied by a recorded tape of layered clarinet loops.

Experimental Music – the Avant-garde

From the 1950s onward, a number of composers have written music that challenges the very notion of what music is. Using new instruments such as the **Theremin**, the **synthesizer** and recording media, they have pushed the boundaries beyond melody and rhythm to create new music using sound as a raw material to be shaped and sculpted. The pieces were either pre-recorded, multi-tracked so they could be manipulated live with a mixer, or a combination of recordings and live parts to be performed alongside each other. Luciano Berio (*Sequenza III*) and Karlheinz Stockhausen (*Kontakte*) were two of the most important explorers of this new sound-world. John Cage was another notable composer in this field, becoming well-known for the use of **chance elements** in his music; *4'33"* relies completely on sounds and noises happening unpredictably. Cage is also known for the music he wrote for **prepared piano**, where items such as screws and bolts are placed between the wires of a piano to create a keyboard of percussive sounds.

WESTERN JAZZ AND POPULAR MUSIC

Jazz

Key features:

*   **Swing rhythm** (or shuffle rhythm) was a popular beat. Other rhythmic styles adopted by jazz musicians include Latin rhythms such as **bossa nova** and **samba**.
*   **Blue notes** are used in the melody and harmony; the 3rd, 5th and 7th degrees of the scale are flattened for greater expression.
*   Many jazz pieces use the **12-bar blues** as both a harmonic and structural element; 12-bar blues use the primary triads in the pattern I–I–I–I–IV–IV–I–I–V–IV–I–I (one chord per bar). For variety, some of these chords would be coloured with, for example, a 7th, or replaced with a different chord (a **substitute chord**). It was common to use the 12-bar blues in a **head arrangement** (main theme or 'head' – some **improvised** solos – head again to finish).
*   Melodies and solos are developed from small motifs called **riffs**.
*   Jazz harmony became increasingly complex as it borrowed chords from the Romantic and Modern composers. There evolved a system of notating these chords in shorthand that was not unlike the Baroque figured bass (e.g., Cm7b5 = C, Eb, Gb, Bb).
*   Improvisation plays a very important role in jazz. Soloists (or a group of soloists) base their improvisations on the **Blues scale** or a **mode** that fits with the underlying chord pattern. Musicians such as Louis Armstrong (trumpet), Charlie Parker (alto saxophone), Oscar Peterson (piano) and Buddy Rich (drums) became known for their **virtuoso** improvisations.
*   New playing techniques were developed; woodwind and brass players found ways to bend pitches with **fall-offs**, and other **portamento** techniques. Brass tone was modified with a variety of **mutes** placed in the bell (e.g., the '**wah-wah**') and players experimented with **growling** into their

instruments as they played. Vocalists improvised as well, using nonsense syllables in a style called **scat singing**.

• Jazz ensembles usually contained a group of melodic **front-line** instruments (saxophones, trumpets, trombones) accompanied by a **rhythm section** of piano, guitar, double bass and drums. Earlier groups had clarinet and cornet as front-line instruments, while rhythm sections used banjo and tuba. Most jazz ensembles were fairly small, except for the big bands, who multiplied the front line instruments for a bigger sound.

Genres, contexts and composers:

The first jazz pieces were the piano rags of Scott Joplin, written around the turn of the 20th century. Ragtime referred to the 'ragged', syncopated right hand part, which was accompanied by a stricter left hand part, often consisting of alternating octaves and chords in a pattern called **stride bass**. Joplin spent part of his life playing in the bars and brothels of St. Louis and Chicago; this association between jazz ensembles and small, intimate venues has continued throughout its history. The first **trad** or **Dixieland** jazz bands appeared in New Orleans, and there are some good reasons for this: firstly New Orleans was a port where many different kinds of music from around the world could be heard. Indeed, most jazz can be said to be a fusion of African rhythm, American gospel and blues and European harmony. Secondly the instruments used in the first Dixie bands were military instruments surplus to requirements after the American Civil War. Besides playing in small clubs, these bands could also play on the move, most famously in funeral processions. Another Dixieland trademark was the collective improvisation, which often resulted in some rather heterophonic counter-melodies.

As jazz spread across America and into Europe in the 1920s, it became less spontaneous and more organized as arrangers wrote out parts for the bands to play. The ensembles grew into **Big Bands**, with tight ensemble work and virtuoso leaders such as Benny Goodman (clarinet) and Glenn Miller (trombone). This was the era of **swing**, which lasted through the 1930s and early 1940s, with the Big Bands making records, radio broadcasts and playing in dance halls.

Economic times were hard after World War II, and jazz bands became smaller again, but their music was faster and more technically demanding with more complex harmonies. This style became known as **Be-bop** and its leading lights were Charlie Parker (alto sax) and Dizzy Gillespie (trumpet). In the 1960s be-bop gave way to **modern** or **cool jazz**, led by Stan Getz (alto sax) and Miles Davis (trumpet). Modern jazz was a logical progression from be-bop with further rises in tempo, technicality, experimentation and harmonic complexity. This marks the point where jazz lost its mass appeal, being replaced by the emergence of rock'n'roll and 'pop' music.

Popular music

Better known as 'pop', from the 1950s to the present day this has been used as a term to describe non-classical music. Like Western classical music, pop has evolved over time; the main difference is that pop has changed and developed much more quickly through hundreds of new styles and fashions – too numerous for detailed discussion here.

Key features:

- Almost all pop music is based around songs with a structure built from sections (**introduction, verse, bridge, chorus, middle eight, instrumental solos, coda**). Bridges and middle eights are sometimes used to bring variety and contrast to the songs.
- Most pop music is in **common time** (4 beats in a bar) with accents on the 2nd and 4th beats (the **backbeat**). However, other time signatures and metres are not entirely forgotten; they sometimes occur as the result of an extended phrase, and in the music of more progressive, experimental bands and artists. **Accents** and **syncopation** are very important rhythmic features in pop music.
- Melodies, riffs and solos are based on the **blues scale** and **modes** (including **pentatonic**, or five-note mode). Performers often decorate their melodies with blue notes, grace notes, pitch-bends and **portamento** (a glide from one note to another).
- Like jazz, the harmonic vocabulary is derived from Western classical music, although most songwriters tend to keep the harmonies fairly simple.
- Although there is no standard line-up for a pop group, many of them feature electric and acoustic guitars, bass guitar, drum kit, keyboards and of course a lead singer. Guitars are often divided into separate **lead** and **rhythm** parts. Many pop styles also call for a **horn section** (typically an alto saxophone, trumpet and trombone), percussion and **backing vocals**. It is also possible to hear orchestral and ethnic instruments playing on pop songs.
- New technology has had a big influence on the development of pop music. Musicians have been quick to exploit new sounds from **synthesizers** and **samplers**; **effects** such as **reverb**, **delay** and **distortion**; and recording methods using tape and computer hard drives and software.
- Pop singers tend to use only the chest and throat areas of the voice, because they offer more power. Some singers also use a variety of other vocal sounds in their music for more expression: shouts, growls, screams and falsetto (a way of reaching higher notes beyond the normal range).

Styles, contexts and composers

Rock'n'roll was the first pop style to emerge in the southern United States in the 1950s. American society at this time was largely conservative in its outlook, and blacks were still being heavily discriminated against by whites. Young artists such as Elvis Presley and Little Richard combined the music they heard around them (white Country Music and black Blues and Gospel) and came up with a new style loved by the teenagers, who listened to the radio, watched television, and could afford to buy records – but the style challenged many long-held values of the older generation. Elvis's rock'n'roll sound, coupled with the new mass media of television, made him a superstar almost overnight.

In the same way that the port of New Orleans was a natural place for jazz to develop, the same is true of Liverpool as a place for John Lennon and Paul McCartney to absorb new influences from America to help them create the early sound of the Beatles. During the 1960s they achieved worldwide acclaim for a series of ground-breaking albums produced by George Martin, who encouraged the band to experiment with different styles and new studio techniques such as multi-track recording, which made it possible to add new parts to those already laid down. Other guitar-based bands such as the Rolling Stones and the Jimi Hendrix Experience achieved similar recognition; Hendrix's innovations in electric guitar technique continue to influence guitarists today.

The late 1960s and 1970s saw new styles emerge. **Reggae** led by Jamaican Bob Marley featured a distinctive off-beat style of rhythm guitar playing called **skanking**. Reggae songs were often about political protest, social struggle and the Rastafarian religion. In the United States the **Soul** sound of Motown Records emerged, a mixture of Blues and Gospel with a powerful, aggressive style of singing called 'secular testifying'. Soul bands were often larger than the standard 3–5 musicians in a pop band, usually adding a horn section and gospel backing singers. James Brown is regarded as one of the pioneers of Soul and his band were known for their tight sound and choreographed dance moves. Other styles, such as Funk and Disco grew out of Soul. New styles of rock appeared: **Progressive Rock**, full of musicianship, experimentation and lengthy songs (Genesis, Pink Floyd); **Punk Rock**, fast, loud distorted guitars, aggressive, full of anger and protest (Sex Pistols, The Clash); **Heavy Metal**, also aggressive with distorted guitars but a more considered approach to song-writing (Led Zeppelin, Black Sabbath). On the pop front the Swedish band Abba achieved global commercial success with effective, catchy songs written by Benny Andersson and Bjorn Ulvaeus.

Hip-hop and Rap

Hip-hop started in the Bronx, New York, in the mid-1970s among the young African-American community and was one of the first pop styles to rely largely on technology rather than live instruments. **Record decks**, **drum machines**, samplers and synthesizers were the main instruments, and were used to provide a looped backing for vocalists who rapped their songs in a mostly spoken style, skilfully using rhythm and phrasing instead of singing. Hip-hop features many distinctive techniques, such as **scratching**, a sound effect created by rapidly moving a vinyl record back and forth on a turntable. Another was **beat boxing**, where the rappers would imitate the sounds and rhythms produced by drum machines and other instruments. **Call and response** chants, which are also found in traditional African music, are also found in several hip-hop songs. Important hip-hop artists include Run–DMC, MC Hammer and Eminem.

WORLD MUSIC

At least one question in Section B will be about music from non-Western cultures, mostly from Asia, Africa, Central and South America and Australasia. While this is potentially a vast amount of music to cover, it is possible to give an overview of the music to have come from these places and cultures. You should carefully listen to and learn the key words and instruments for each culture, as many of them are unusual and distinctive in both name and sound.

India

The oldest Indian music is known as **Raga** (also called Indian Classical Music) and dates back over two thousand years. It was associated with the Hindu religion and performed at ceremonies as well as for pure entertainment. Raga is also the name given to the scales used to improvise melodies; like Western scales they exist both in ascending and descending forms, but in Ragas the pitches used in them can be very different. Raga scales were created for certain times of day or seasons; many have been written for particular moods or occasions (e.g., reflective evenings, bravery or a wedding). Rhythms are based upon patterns known as **Tala**; they often have odd metres and are also used as a basis for improvisation. These two elements are accompanied by a **drone** of 2–3 principal notes from the Raga scale. The three typical instruments used in a Raga performance are listed below:

- **Sitar** – a plucked guitar-like instrument, with 7 main strings and several **sympathetic** strings, which vibrate when the main strings are played: this is what gives the sitar its bright, 'twangy' sound. It has a small body and a long neck with frets. The sitar plays and improvises on the raga scale.

- **Tabla** – a pair of single-headed drums played with the hands and fingers. They play and improvise on the Tala rhythm.
- **Tambura** – a smaller plucked string instrument with 4 strings; it is played in a vertical position. The tambura plays the drone.

A typical Raga performance contains four important structural points, each with its own identifiable musical features:

- **Alap** – the notes of the Raga scale are slowly introduced one by one, with no fixed rhythm or tempo.
- **Jor** – a regular pulse is added to the Alap.
- **Gat** – the tabla enter, improvising on the Tala rhythm. The sitar improvises on the Raga scale.
- **Jhalla** – the tempo increases and the rhythms become more complex to create an exciting finish.

Other melodic instruments can be used in place of the sitar: the **sarod** is also a plucked string instrument, but has no frets; the **sarangi** is played with a bow and capable of a wide range of vibrato and sliding effects. The sarangi is also closely associated with Indian vocal music.

Another style of Indian music with both a long history and recent popularity is **Bhangra**, a lively folk dance originating from the Punjab region on the border between India and Pakistan. The main element in Bhangra is the dotted, shuffle-like rhythm of the **dhol**, a large double-headed drum played with wooden sticks. More recently Bhangra has been fused with Western hip-hop, achieving wider popularity in the United Kingdom and North America.

China

Traditional Chinese music dates back well over two thousand years and was used for a variety of purposes, including dance and entertainment at the imperial court as well as accompanying Chinese opera. Most of the melodies are based on the **pentatonic** scale, and are either performed solo, or in small groups in a **heterophonic** texture (i.e., each performer plays the melody, with small but noticeable differences). There is sometimes a simple harmony part in parallel 3rds or 4ths. Ensembles are often made up of four sections: a woodwind section with **bamboo flutes**; a bowed string section with, for example, an **erhu** (similar to a violin but with only one string); a plucked string instrument such as the **guzheng** or **pipa**; and a percussion section with drums and the brash-sounding cymbals typical of the region. Songs are usually sung in a thin-sounding voice, often using the falsetto range.

In the years following the Communist Revolution in 1949 marches were written, often to be sung with words celebrating the successes of the government.

Japan

There are a number of similarities with Chinese music in terms of when and where it was used, largely because Japan was also ruled for centuries by an imperial system. Like China a pentatonic scale was used in traditional melodies, but there are two different versions in Japan, called **yo** and **in**:

- Yo scale – has no semitones (e.g., D–F–G–A–C–(D), or D–E–G–A–B–(D)) and was thought to sound 'bright'.
- In scale – includes semitones (e.g. D–E♭–G–A–B♭–(D)) and sounded 'dark'.

Bamboo flutes are also present; in Japan this flute is called the **shakuhachi** and was played by court and folk musicians, and Buddhist monks who played it as part of their meditation. The most important folk music traditions in Japan include:

- **Minyo**, solo songs accompanied by one or two **shamisen**, a plucked string instrument with 3 strings, and a **koto**, a zither-like instrument very similar to the guzheng.
- **Biwa hoshi**, a form of narrative song featuring a solo performer telling epic tales in a partly sung, partly spoken manner. The performer accompanies him or herself on the biwa, another plucked string instrument, this one resembling a lute, played with a large triangular plectrum.
- **Taiko** – a large, barrel-shaped drum in various sizes played with a pair of thick wooden sticks. They are often played in percussion ensembles whose rhythmic playing is both acrobatic and energetic. Taiko drums were also used in the past to communicate messages on the battlefield.

Indonesia

The many islands of Indonesia are best known for their **Gamelan** orchestras, a centuries-old tradition used to accompany anything from religious ceremonies to plays and puppet dramas. Most of the instruments in Gamelan orchestras are of the tuned percussion variety, and made of metal or wooden bars and played with wooden mallets (indeed, the word 'Gamelan' literally means 'struck by many'):

- **Saron** – one of the smaller 'metallophones'; they play a series of basic repeated melodies.
- **Bonang** – slightly larger than the saron, they play an off-beat counter-melody that interlocks with the on-beat saron part.
- **Gongs** – the largest tuned percussion, they play an important role marking the start and end points of each repetition.

Other instruments that can be heard in Gamelan music are bamboo flute, fiddle and voice. The music is directed by a drummer, who plays a double-headed hand drum and signals tempo changes during a performance. Gamelan music has a hypnotic sound, with sudden changes in tempo and dynamics. Many pieces use a pentatonic scale called **slendro**; the exact tuning varies from one island to another and is in all cases quite different to the Western pentatonic scale; the closest equivalent Western notes are C–D–F–G–A. Another, more chromatic scale, known as **pelog** is also regularly used (D–E♭–F–G♯–A– B♭– C), but many ensembles lack the 4th and 7th notes, so there are several pentatonic pelog pieces in which these are omitted.

Latin America

A very diverse range of styles and genres have evolved from the Spanish and Portuguese colonization of Central and South America, but it is also worth noting that the music of Spain and Portugal itself resulted from a mixture of influences from Moorish occupation to French troubadours.

Argentina is best known for the **Tango**, a dance that was, once again, a fusion of styles introduced into a port city, this time Buenos Aires. Tango contains rhythmic and melodic elements from Eastern Europe (polka and mazurka), Spain (flamenco) and Cuba (habanera). The 4/4 metre often has a distinctive offbeat accent after the 4th beat, commonly emphasized by a snare drum roll into the next bar. The other distinctive sound is the melody that is played on the **bandoneon**, a type of concertina controlled by buttons rather than piano keys.

The Andes mountain range covers several South American countries, including Bolivia, Columbia, Peru and Chile. **Andean** folk music features indigenous instruments such as the **panpipes**, as well as the imported Spanish guitar.

Panpipes are made from cylindrical reeds arranged in rows and tuned to pentatonic and diatonic scales. Folk melodies are often split between two panpipe players, a technique known as a **hocket**. Hocketing is found in other times and cultures, but it is a typical feature of Andean music. Bands consisting of panpipes and drums frequently play at weddings and fiestas.

Brazil is synonymous with the **samba**, a party dance that has almost become a national culture on its own. It is closely associated with the **Carnival** in Rio de Janeiro, during which **samba schools** compete to have the best floats, dancing and music. Beneath the solid up-tempo 2/4 metre, a large group of different percussion instruments (known as the **bateria**) beat out a rhythmic counterpoint of accents and syncopated patterns. The bateria usually consists of a **surdo** (bass drums), **caixa** (snare drums), **cuica** (tom-toms), **tamborims** (similar in size to a tambourine, but it has no jingles), African agogo bells and shakers. In addition some bands have guitars, trumpets and singers.

Music in **Mexico** has a long and diverse history, but of all the genres the country is known for, the sound of the **Mariachi** is the most familiar. Mariachi bands typically contain trumpets, violins and three different sizes of guitar; besides the regular guitar there is the larger **guitarron** and the smaller **vihuela**. Sometimes a harp is used, and all the mariachis are singers. They are usually hired for weddings and other special occasions because most of their traditional songs are about love and romance. In other genres, many Mexican songs have become known around the world (e.g., *La Cucaracha* and, more recently, *La Bamba*) and the country has produced several internationally renowned artists such as the operatic tenor Placido Domingo and the Latino-rock guitarist Carlos Santana.

The islands of the Caribbean are a perfect example of how different cultural traditions have been fused together to create new styles and genres. Nowhere is this truer than **Cuba**, where European melody and harmony combined with African percussion and polyrhythm to create many Latin dances:

- **Habanera** – a slow 2/4 style. The main beats are decorated with syncopations, dotted rhythms and triplets. The habanera influenced modern composers such as Ravel and developed into the tango in Argentina.
- **Salsa** – a fusion of several Cuban dances, including **son** and **mambo**, and uses a distinctive syncopated 4/4 rhythm called **son clave**. Salsa has a trademark percussion section of bongos, congas, claves and timbales. Typical salsa bands also feature trumpets, trombones, piano (often played in octaves) and bass guitar.
- **Cha-cha-cha** – a less syncopated dance in 4/4 that took its name from the rhythm made on the dance floor by the dancers!

On the island of **Trinidad** oil drums are recycled into **steel pans** that form an important part of the **Calypso** sound. The top of the oil drum is hammered into several flat spots of various sizes to obtain the notes of the chromatic scale. Steel bands are made up of a 'choir' of pans named after the vocal ranges (soprano, alto, etc.), plus a percussion section. Most calypso melody and harmony is again derived from Europe; melodies are mostly step-wise with a few leaps and chromatic decorations, and the harmony is mostly primary diatonic chords. Although these bands are best known for calypso, they also play a wide variety of other styles, including jazz, popular tunes and even classical music.

Middle East

Although Middle Eastern music covers a vast area from Afghanistan across to Morocco in North Africa, and many local traditions are still continued, the spread of Islam from the Arabian Peninsula was a strong unifying factor. One of the most familiar sounds of the Islamic world is the call to prayer sung by a **muezzin** five times daily. However, music is also used for dance and entertainment. The melodic scales, similar to those found in Indian music, have up to 24 notes in one octave, which often results in some subtle changes of pitch. Ensembles typically have four players, offering opportunities for improvisation. Middle Eastern music is mostly monophonic in texture, accompanied by simple percussion such as drums and finger cymbals. Rhythm can be complex with odd metres, accents and syncopations, and the patterns are memorized. The best-known instrument is the **oud**, a lute-like instrument with 4–6 strings. There are also woodwind instruments; the **ney** is similar to the flute and made from cane, and various oboe-like **double-reed** instruments, which sound bright and harsh, can also be heard across the region.

Africa

It is usual to divide African music into two main geographical regions, Northern and sub-Saharan Africa. The music of the North has been influenced by a succession of different civilisations and occupying powers: for example, Ancient Egypt and the Greeks and Romans. But this music is now most closely related to Middle Eastern culture. Music in sub-Saharan Africa is mostly functional: work songs, music to mark births, marriages or deaths, music for spiritual ceremony and ritual, and so on. This music is best known for its rhythmic features: odd metres, syncopation, layering of different patterns over each other (**polyrhythm**) are all frequently heard. Ensembles are led by a **Master Drummer**, who sets the tempo and calls the changes in the music. Master Drummers are highly respected within their tribes. There is a vast array of African percussion instruments, drums, bells, xylophones and shakers. The **Djembe** is a single-headed hand drum with a wooden shell; its goblet shape allows it to play a variety of different tones from a high slap to a more resonant bass. Another widely used instrument is the **talking drum**, a double-headed drum with strings connecting the two heads, whose pitch can be precisely altered by squeezing the strings as the drum is played. Many African languages are very melodic and the talking drum is used for communication as well as for music. There are some melodic instruments resembling flutes, trumpets and violins, but it is the voice which is the most important. There is a rich variety of song to be found across the whole region, often sung in a **call and response** texture with simple harmony in 3rds. Other vocal techniques heard are **melisma** and **yodelling**, where the singer rapidly switches between head voice and chest voice.

Europe

There are many forms of folk music across Europe which over time has regularly influenced Western Classical and other traditional music around the world. Most of this music consists of songs and dances as typified by that of the **United Kingdom**. British folk music is modal; melodies tend to have a one-octave range and are accompanied by simple diatonic chords. Some instruments have become associated with specific regions of the country: Scottish bagpipes, the Welsh harp and the Irish fiddle and bodhran, a large, shallow drum played with both ends of a single drumstick. English folk music includes a number of different genres, including Morris Dancing, sea shanties and the brass bands that developed during the Industrial Revolution. **Spain**'s music of the **flamenco** has become known across the world. The main elements of flamenco are the rapid picking and strumming techniques of the guitar, the emotional and high-pitched singing style, and the percussion, much of which is performed by the dancers through stomping, handclapping and castanets. In **Eastern Europe**, many other dance forms still exist, such as the fast 2/4 **polka** and the more moderate 3/4 **mazurka**.

Australia

The music of the Aboriginal people is among the oldest in the world, and instantly recognizable because of the iconic **didgeridoo**. The didgeridoo is traditionally made from a cylindrical piece of hardwood and produces a drone that can be modified by the performer using vocal and breathing techniques. The drone can be sustained with **circular breathing** for 40–50 minutes without a break. The voice can be used whilst playing to mimic animal calls such as the **kookaburra** or **dingo**. The didgeridoo is still important in Aboriginal culture and is played for ceremonies, songs and dances. It is often accompanied by **clapsticks**, a pair of wooden sticks hit together like claves. Aboriginal singing is characterized by a complex combination of melodic chants, hisses, shouts, grunts and wails.

Fusion

The IB Music examination often features an extract in which elements from more than one culture can be heard. In the late 20th century, as knowledge and enjoyment of world music has become more widespread, musicians have been influenced by an increasing range of ideas and techniques from other styles and cultures. This has given rise to a large amount of 'fusion music' – a hybrid of two (or more) distinct styles or cultural traditions. The sheer diversity of styles makes them hard to categorize, but here are a few notable examples for study and further listening:

- **African Sanctus** – a Mass written by David Fanshawe in the 1970s, which combines a four-part SATB choir with a rock band and recordings of traditional African music made by the composer on a journey up the River Nile.
- **Afro Celt Sound System** – a group formed in the 1990s, they blend electronic dance rhythms with traditional Irish and West African music.
- **Graceland** – an album released by Paul Simon in 1986, bringing a number of Southern African musical traditions to a global audience and combining them with Western pop and rock.
- **Shang Shang Typhoon** – a Japanese band formed in the 1980s, which blend traditional minyo singing with Western pop, rock and reggae. The band leader, in the true spirit of fusion music, plays what he calls a 'sangen', a banjo fitted with strings from a shamisen.
- **Bhangra** – a fusion of Punjabi music and songs with Western pop, rock and dance elements. Some of Bhangra's best known acts are Golden Star UK, Alaap and Heera.

SAMPLE QUESTIONS

The standard wording for Section B questions is: "Analyse, examine and discuss in detail what you hear in this extract." You may answer these in continuous prose or detailed bullet points and you should allow around

30 minutes to complete each question. Remember that marks are awarded for the following:

- Describing musical elements (instruments/voices, tempo, rhythm, melody, harmony, tonality, texture).
- Using the correct terminology when describing the musical elements.
- Outlining the structure of the music.
- Outlining the context of the music (period, date, composer, genre, purpose).

Here are the web links for some practice questions for you to try: suggested answers can found on **page 122:**

1. https://www.youtube.com/watch?v=vFZZMF7SRRo (0'00"–2'13" score included) Byrd – *Ave verum corpus*
2. https://www.youtube.com/watch?v=gGnv23IRDvM (0'00"–2'15" score not included) Shostakovich *Symphony No.7 1st movement* 'The Invasion episode'
3. https://www.youtube.com/watch?v=W4_aE1CVr1s (0'00"–2'24" score not included) Schumann *Piano Quartet 3rd movement*
4. https://www.youtube.com/watch?v=NKXFdT14DIE (0'00"–2'23" score included) Beethoven *Symphony No.7 2nd movement*
5. https://www.youtube.com/watch?v=h5eyeDYNkkQ (0'00"–2'15" score not included) Handel *Messiah no's 14–17*
6. https://www.youtube.com/watch?v=hWNZo8iJ5EQ (0'00"–2'04" score not included) Nat Adderley *Work Song*
7. https://www.youtube.com/watch?v=p-Y6RArekGc (0'00"–2'04" score not included) Africando *Betece*
8. https://www.youtube.com/watch?v=LL-E8jfslr8 (0'00"–2'04" score not included) Yu Cheng *Springtime on the Tianshan Mountains*
9. https://www.youtube.com/watch?v=wk3NPfPPIyM (0'00"–2'00" score not included) LeMoyne-Owen College *Chikuyu*

These web links give away some of the answers for the contextual element of the question, such as the composer or the culture. Therefore, you should try to find some extracts from other sources where you will have to work out these factors from the musical elements you hear.

GLOSSARY

A cappella – Literally 'in/of the chapel'. Unaccompanied vocal music, either sacred or secular.

Alberti bass – A type of broken chord accompaniment used frequently, but not exclusively, in Classical period piano pieces.

Anacrusis – A group of unaccented notes prior to the first full bar of a phrase or piece. The equivalent term in Pop and Jazz is a **pick-up**.

Anapaestic rhythm – In poetry, a word describing two short syllables followed by a longer one. Rhythmically this can be seen, e.g., as 2 semiquavers followed by a quaver.

Antiphony – A texture in which different groups of musicians have alternating passages.

Answer – In a fugue, the repeat of the subject by a second voice, usually in a new but related key. An exact (but transposed) repeat of the subject is known as a *real answer*, whereas a modified repeat is a *tonal answer*.

Aria – A piece for solo voice, usually with accompaniment. Most commonly found in operas, oratorios or cantatas.

Arabesque – In melody, an elaborate florid phrase.

Arco – An instruction to string players to play with their bows, usually after a **pizzicato** passage. *See* **Pizzicato**.

Augmentation – A device for developing melodic material in a piece; the lengthening of the rhythmic values of a given phrase or passage of music. *See also* **Diminution**.

Augmented 6th – A chromatic chord based on the flattened 6th of the scale, with the outer notes forming the interval of an augmented 6th. E.g., in C major its root would be A♭, plus C, E♭ and F♯. This is known as the German 6th, and there are some variants on this affecting the 5th of the chord; the Italian 6th omits the 5th altogether (i.e., A♭–C–F♯), and the French 6th replaces the 5th with a 4th (i.e., A♭–C–D–F♯).

Auxiliary note – A non-chord note that is a variant of the **passing note**; instead of moving away to another pitch, it returns to the one from which it came, e.g., A–G–A.

Binary form – A musical structure with two distinct sections, which are often repeated (i.e., AABB).

Bitonal(ity) – In modern harmony and/or tonality, where two different chords/keys are heard at the same time.

Blues scale – A scale using blue notes, e.g., C–E♭–F–G♭–G–B♭–C; the blue notes were originally flattened to help create the sad feel of the American Blues, but the scale is used widely today in styles and cultures around the world.

Cadence – The final chords or notes at the end of a phrase. The main harmonic cadences are: **Perfect**, V–I (sounds finished); **Imperfect**, 2 chords ending on V (sounds unfinished); **Interrupted**, V–VI/any unexpected chord (avoids a finish by not moving to chord I); **Plagal**, IV–I (sounds finished, the 'Amen' cadence in church music); **Phrygian**, IVb–V (an imperfect cadence for minor keys sometimes found in the Renaissance and Baroque periods).

Cadenza – A brilliant virtuoso passage for a soloist, typically in a concerto.

Call and response – A type of antiphony where phrases from a solo 'caller' alternate with responses from a group of singers/players. Call and response is an important feature of traditional African music.

Canon – A contrapuntal piece or passage where two or more parts have the melody in exact imitation, each entering a few beats after the other.

Chordal – A texture consisting exclusively of chords; they can further described as sustained, detached or broken chords.

Chromatic – Literally 'coloured', a note or chord that does not belong to the prevailing key of the music. It can be used to describe both melody and harmony.

Circle of 5ths – A progression of chords or key changes wherein each new root or key is a 5th above or below the preceding one.

Coda – The closing passage of a piece, song or movement.

Codetta – The closing passage of a *section* in a larger structure.

Coloratura – An elaborate melody, particularly in operatic singing of the 18th and 19th centuries, with runs, wide leaps and trills.

Conjunct – Melodic movement up or down by one note; also known as **stepwise movement**.

Consonance – Two or more notes that harmonize without tension, a concord.

Contrapuntal – A texture consisting of two or more melodies sounding together. *See* **Polyphonic**.

Contrary motion – A texture in which two or more parts move in opposite directions away from or towards each other.

Counter-melody – An extra melody heard in counterpoint against the main melody of the passage. In **fugue** this is known as a **counter-subject**.

Cross-rhythm – A passage in which the rhythm deliberately runs against the main pulse/metre of the piece.

Dactylic rhythm – In poetry, a word describing a long syllable followed by two shorter ones. Rhythmically this can be seen, e.g., as a quaver followed by 2 semiquavers.

Delay – A time-based effect that adds one or more echoes to the part being sung or played.

Development – The middle section of Sonata Form, or any section where thematic material is moulded and shaped through a variety of keys.

Diatonic – A melodic or harmonic passage or piece that uses only the notes of the prevailing key, with no accidentals.

Diminished 7th – A striking chromatic chord built up entirely with minor 3rds, e.g., G#–B–D–F. Notice the outer notes in this example form the interval of the same value.

Diminution – A device for developing melodic material in a piece; the shortening of the rhythmic values of a given phrase or passage of music. *See also* **Augmentation**.

Disjunct – The opposite of **Conjunct**; melodic movement by leaping to notes more than one step away.

Dissonance – Two or more notes that clash, a discord creating tension. Up until 1900 most composers prepared and resolved dissonances, but since then they have been used with ever-greater freedom on their own.

Distortion – An effect commonly used on electric guitar, but can also be used on any instrument or voice; it involves deliberately making the sound 'dirty' by overdriving the amplifier's gain control.

Drone – One or two fixed notes heard as a continuous bass, especially on bagpipes. Heard often in folk music and sometimes in Western Classical music.

Drum machine – An electronic instrument used to play and create percussive sounds and rhythm patterns by mechanical or digital means.

Enharmonic change – The changing of the *name* of a given note, but not the actual *pitch*, e.g., C# to D♭. Composers use enharmonic change to effect clever and subtle modulations.

Episode – In **fugue**, a passage of music used to separate and modulate between entries of the main fugue subject.

Exposition – The first section in a Sonata Form movement, and also the name given to the opening of a **fugue**.

False relation – In harmony, a dissonance where 2 different versions of the same note are heard in close proximity in *different* parts. E.g., a G natural in the soprano heard in the same/similar place as a G# in the tenor.

Fantasia – Name given to a variety of pieces through Western music history. Generally, it refers to a piece in which form is less important compared to those with a more definite structure.

Fugal – A polyphonic texture which uses characteristics found in **fugue**. *See* **Fugue**.

Fugue – A **contrapuntal** musical form that begins with a statement of the **subject** (main theme) followed by entries in other parts using the same subject. As the second part states the subject (known as the **answer**), the first moves on to the **counter-subject**, a new theme, in counterpoint with the subject. The opening of a fugue is known as the **exposition**; after each part has made its first entry, the fugue proceeds through further entries in related keys until the tonic is reestablished towards the end.

Genre – Literally a type of composition, such as the opera, the concerto, etc.

Grace note – A decorative note with no time value of its own (indicated as a small note with a line crossed through the stem) which is 'crushed' in just before the main note it is linked to. Also known as an **acciaccatura**.

Harmonic rhythm – The rate or frequency of chord changes in a passage of music. Harmonic rhythm often speeds up on the approach to a cadence or a modulation.

Heterophonic – A texture in which slightly different versions of the melody are played simultaneously.

Hexatonic – Music that uses a scale of 6 notes.

Homophonic – A texture that consists of either a melody and accompaniment, or a passage in which the parts move together in the same rhythm (this is also known as a **chordal** or **homorhythmic** texture).

Homorhythmic – A texture in which all the parts move forward using the same rhythm.

Imitation – In texture, the more or less exact copying of a phrase in one part/voice by another. Exact imitation is known as a **canon**.

Inversion – The turning upside-down of a melodic figure, interval, chord or pedal point. If a **triad** has its 3rd or 5th as the bass note, it is said to be inverted.

Lied (plural **Lieder**) – The German word for song, particularly those written for voice and piano during the 19th century to Romantic poems.

Mediant modulation – A change of key where the new key is a 3rd above or below the old; e.g., E major to C major. This is also known as **tertiary modulation**.

Melisma – In vocal music, a passage in which several notes are sung to one syllable of the words. *See* **Syllabic**.

Metre – The pattern of the beats in a given bar; e.g., 3/4 time is usually arranged as strong-weak-weak triple metre.

Mixer – A device used to combine and process signals/sounds from a variety of different sources.

Modal – *See* **Modes**

Modes – In ancient Greece, when the notes of the scale were worked out, the Greeks used them in 7 different ways, all of which can be found on the white notes of the keyboard, each starting on a different note and each with its own characteristic sound. E.g., A–B–C–D–E–F–G–A is Aeolian mode, also known as the natural minor scale; notice that the leading note G is natural and not sharp as it would be in the harmonic minor scale. In tonal music only two 'modes' exist – major and minor, but the Greek modes have had an influence on music across time, place and culture.

Modulation – A technical term used to describe a change of key in a piece of music.

Monophonic – A texture that consists of a solo melodic line with no accompaniment.

Motif – A short melodic fragment the composer uses to help create a complete theme/melody.

Neapolitan 6th – A chromatic chord using the flattened supertonic (II) triad in first inversion. E.g., in E minor, the supertonic triad is F♯–A–C, which is then flattened and inverted to become A–C–F.

Neo-classical – A 20th century style that drew on the techniques and styles of the Baroque and Classical periods, blending them with modern approaches to elements, such as harmony and rhythm.

Oblique motion – A texture with a moving part(s) against a static part(s).

Ostinato – A persistently repeated melody, bass, chord pattern or rhythm; it is often a significant feature of the piece. In Pop and Jazz this is known as a **riff**.

Parallel motion – A texture in which the parts move in a similar direction, but using the same interval between them: e.g., a melody in parallel 3rds or a chain of parallel 7th chords.

Pedal point – ('Pedal') A harmonic device in which a fixed sustained or repeated note is heard whilst the chords above it change. Pedals are usually placed in the bass part but can also appear in the top line (inverted pedal) or in a middle part (inner pedal). Pedals can also be described according to which degree of the scale they are on, most commonly the dominant or the tonic.

Pentatonic – Music that uses a scale of 5 notes, commonly found in different cultures around the world. A pentatonic scale can be found by playing on the black notes of a keyboard.

Pick-up – *See* **Anacrusis**.

Pivot chord – In modulation, a chord that belongs to both the old and the new key, enabling a smooth transition.

Pizzicato – (*Pizz.*) An instruction to string players to pluck the strings instead of using their bows. *See* **Arco**.

Polarized – A texture that features a wide gap between the melodic parts and the bass.

Polychoral – Music written for 2 or more groups of performers who are often placed in different parts of the performing space.

Polyphonic – Literally 'many tunes'; a texture consisting of two or more melodies sounding together. An alternative term is **contrapuntal**; in the past this term referred to instrumental music, and polyphonic to vocal music. Today, these terms are used freely to describe all musical genres.

Polyrhythm – Different rhythms used simultaneously in different parts.

Question and answer – In melody, a term used to describe a pair of successive phrases which are both similar and different to each other; e.g., their rhythms are similar but each phrase moves in a different direction.

Recapitulation – The final section of the Sonata Form structure. *See* **Sonata Form**.

Reverb – Short for 'reverberation', the reflections of sound in a space, e.g., a hall or room. Also a studio effect which places a recorded part in a space that can be specified and shaped.

Riff – *See* **Ostinato**.

Ritornello (return) – A musical structure, first used in the late Baroque period, which alternates a main section (the ritornello) with a series of episodes that often use similar musical ideas, a lighter texture, new keys and solo passages.

Rondo form – A musical structure with one principal recurring section, which is alternated with a succession of contrasting episodes. In letter form this is expressed as ABACADA, etc.

Rounded Binary form – A musical structure with two distinct sections, A and B; however the B section contains a shortened reminder of A near the end. Not to be confused with **ternary form**, which features a complete reprise of the A section.

Sample – A short digitally recorded musical idea or sound effect frequently used in music production and composition today.

Sampler – An electronic instrument used to digitally record and manipulate **samples**.

Scotch snap – A rhythmic device typically comprising a semiquaver followed by a dotted quaver (i.e., the reverse of the more common dotted quaver-semiquaver figure), giving the rhythm a 'jerky' feel. Popular in Scottish folk music, it is also found in France, where it is known as the *Lombardic rhythm*.

Secondary dominant – A dominant chord that does not belong to the prevailing key of a passage. E.g., in C major the primary dominant chord is G, whereas a D major triad would be called a secondary dominant.

Sequence – The repetition of a musical passage at a higher or lower pitch. Sequences can be used in the development of either melodic or harmonic material, and passages can be described as melodic or harmonic sequences.

Sforzando (*sfz*) – A dynamic marking asking for a note/chord to be played with 'force'. *Sfp* is a sforzando immediately followed by *piano* (soft).

Similar motion – A texture in which the parts move in the same direction. *See also* **Parallel motion**.

Sonata Form – Tonality-based musical structure often used in the first movement of a sonata, symphony, concerto, etc. First used in the Classical period. The 3 sections typically run as follows: **exposition**, with 2 sets of themes (**subjects**) in 2 related but different keys (e.g., tonic and dominant); **development**, where the themes are explored through a variety of different keys; **recapitulation**, with the 2 sets of themes now presented in the tonic key only. Sonata Form is also used in other movements. Over time Sonata Form has evolved into more complex variants but the three main sections are usually still discernible.

Sotto voce – 'Under the voice'. A dramatic lowering of the volume of the voices or instruments, in order to achieve a hushed tone.

Stepwise movement – *See* **Conjunct**

Stretto – In a **polyphonic** or fugal piece, a passage in which the imitating parts are drawn together so that they enter one after the other more closely than before.

Strophic – A musical form in vocal music in which each verse of the words is set to the same music: e.g., a hymn.

Subject – The name given to a set of themes in a Sonata Form movement; also the name given to the main theme in a **fugue**.

Suspension – In harmony, a dissonance where a note in a concord is held over into the next chord, creating a brief clash which is then usually resolved downward by a step to form another concord. These 3 stages are called preparation, suspension and resolution.

Swing rhythm – A jazz rhythm in which pairs of quavers are played in an unequal long–short pattern, rather than as two notes of equal length. Also known as the 'shuffle' rhythm.

Syllabic – In vocal music, a passage in which each syllable of the words is set to single notes. *See* **Melisma**.

Symphony – A sonata for orchestra usually, but not always, cast in 4 movements; fast, slow, dance, fast.

Syncopation – A rhythmic device in which the emphasis is on the off-beat notes between the main pulse of the music.

Synthesizer – An electronic instrument that can be used to create and manipulate waveforms and/or samples.

Ternary form – A musical structure with 3 sections; the outer sections are the same or similar, with the middle section acting as a contrast. This form is often expressed in letters as ABA, or ABA[1] if the reprise of A is sufficiently different.

Tertiary modulation – *See* **Mediant modulation**.

Tessitura – A term that describes where a musical part sits in the register of the given instrument/voice (high, low or medium).

Texture – A musical element that describes the way in which different parts playing together relate to each other. *See also* **Monophonic**, **Homophonic**, **Polyphonic**, **Contrapuntal**, **Heterophonic**, **Antiphony** and **Polarized**.

Theremin – Eerie-sounding electronic instrument played by moving the hands around two aerials.

Through-composed – A musical structure that consists of sections, each with its own musical material that is not repeated elsewhere: i.e., ABCD, etc.

Tierce de Picardie – A tonic major ending to what is otherwise a minor key piece or passage.

Tremolo (trembling) – The rapid reiteration of a note/chord. E.g., on a violin this can be done by quickly moving the bow back and forth. Tremolo can be played on other instruments by rapidly alternating 2 notes, e.g., piano or woodwinds.

Triad – A 3-note chord built from 3rds, e.g., C–E–G.

Trill – A melodic decoration consisting of two rapidly alternated stepwise notes.

Tritone – A dissonant interval comprising 3 whole tones (e.g., F–B).

Turn – Melodic ornament whereby a single 'main' note becomes a 4-note figure, literally turning above and below itself by step. E.g., a turn centred on a D would be played as E–D–C–D.

Una corda – Also known as the soft pedal and found on the left of the 3 grand piano pedals. When pressed it shifts the whole action to the right so that the hammers strike fewer strings, resulting in a slightly softer and duller tone.

Variation – A musical form in which a theme (either borrowed or specially written) is presented in a series of different musical guises: e.g., with different rhythms or harmonies. This can be represented in letters as A–A[1]–A[2]–A[3], etc.

Virtuoso – A performer with incredible technical skills.

Whole tone scale – A scale built entirely from whole tones: e.g., C–D–E–F#–G#–A#–C.

SUGGESTED ANSWERS
FOR SAMPLE QUESTIONS

Section A

The following answer to Question 1 from the *Dances of Galánta* practice questions was written under timed conditions. Even though the candidate has used continuous prose on this occasion, remember that you can write your answer in whatever format you prefer, as long as your content successfully answers the question. Some annotated examiner comments have also been included to give you an idea of what they are looking for when assessing a candidate's work.

Béla Bartók once wrote: "If I were to name the composer whose works are the most perfect embodiment of the Hungarian spirit, I would answer, Kodály." Discuss this statement with clear reference to **at least three** passages in *Dances of Galánta*.

Answer:

Although it was written for a symphony orchestra, Kodály's Dances of Galánta *embodies the Hungarian spirit in a number of significant musical ways.*[1]

Probably the most important musical aspect was his use of the Gypsy 'verbunkos' dance style, which was used to recruit young men into the Hungarian army in the 18th and 19th centuries. The music was divided into two main sections, slow and fast. The dignified[2] *slow dance starting at b50 is played as a clarinet solo, a reminder of the similar single reed instrument*[3] *found in Gypsy bands. The melody is 16 bars long with regular phrasing, and is borrowed from an original Gypsy dance, although Kodály has changed the original quaver and semiquaver rhythms into something more suitable for the slow verbunkos, with dotted rhythms in every bar, many ending in flamboyant turn-like triplet figures.*[4] *Another*

---

[1] A very brief introduction rephrasing the question. Do not be drawn into writing a long introduction describing Kodály or the origins of the piece: writing about the music is the priority!

[2] A well-chosen adjective helps to convey the mood of the music.

[3] The candidate has not remembered the exact name of the instrument (the *tárogató*), but would still gain credit for describing it.

[4] Excellent knowledge and detailed musical description.

Hungarian feature is that the melody is built from a 2-bar phrase (bb50-51) which is then repeated in a descending sequence. Like many of the Gypsy tunes used in this piece this theme starts in one key and ends in another; in this example E minor, ending in A minor on a tierce de Picardie (b65).

The second section[5] in a verbunkos dance was always quicker and wilder as can be seen in the Allegro melody (bb236-241). In the tonic key of the piece (A minor), the melody in the violins is an irregular 6-bar phrase, mostly syncopated with a semiquaver flourish in the 6th bar, and is quite repetitive as Kodály goes on to vary and re-score this melody e.g. b276 in D minor, in parallel 6ths (upper strings and woodwind) and an extension to the semiquaver flourish resulting in a single 3/4 bar amongst the prevailing 2/4 metre.[6]

A third,[7] even quicker dance is heard from bb443-450. Like the theme at b236 it is built from a 2-bar phrase (bb443-444) – a syncopated falling octave leap followed by descending semiquaver flourishes. In the next bars (bb445-446 1st violin) the leap is the same but the semiquavers stop short on the 2nd beat, and bb447-448 are an exact repeat of the original 2-bar phrase. Finally, (bb449-450) the semiquaver flourishes take over and lead upwards into a repeat of the whole 8-bar phrase.

Other Hungarian features include the use of modes e.g. Dorian on A bb1-5 (the F♯ is the raised 6th degree in the Dorian scale). Furthermore the return of the slow dance (from b50) at b229-233 is now heard in the Gypsy Dominant scale on B♭, with its distinctive raised 4th (E♮). Some of the other melodies also feature expressive dissonant intervals e.g. b111 1st violin; the G-F♭ augmented 2nd gives this melody the Hungarian sound of the harmonic minor scale.[8]

In conclusion, Kodály has successfully blended elements of the Hungarian Gypsy verbunkos style with Western symphonic methods to create an art music that truly embodies the Hungarian spirit.[9]

The following answer to Question 4 from the Brandenburg Concerto no. 2 practice questions was also written under timed conditions. Here, the candidate has used a mixture of continuous prose and bullet points. Again, some annotated examiner comments have been included.

---

[5] The candidate is using the verbunkos slow/fast sections to not only cover the required 3 passages, but also to continue the main line of argument in their answer.

[6] The example illustrating the point is precisely located in the score and clearly explained using the correct terminology.

[7] Again, continuing the line of argument.

[8] Notice how the candidate uses this paragraph to tie together the other Hungarian features they remembered.

[9] A conclusion is not entirely necessary here; this might be better off as part of the introduction.

Discuss the changing relationship between the solo, ripieno and continuo parts across each of the three movements of Brandenburg Concerto no. 2. Refer in detail to specific passages of music.[10]

Answer:

Bach's Brandenburg Concerto no. 2 features 3 instrumental groups; the 4 soloists (tromba, recorder, oboe and violin), ripieno strings, and the continuo (cello and harpsichord). These groups are used by Bach in a variety of combinations as the piece progresses.[11]

In the 1st movement the ripieno share in the playing of the main ritornello theme as it returns throughout the movement:[12]

- *bb1-8 – ritornello theme played by soloists and ripieno violins. The cello and violone (an instrument similar to the double bass) have their own semiquaver theme in counterpoint at the same time.*
- *bb15-16 – a brief 2-bar tutti: a motif from the ritornello theme is played by 3 of the soloists and ripieno 1st violins. The semiquaver cello/violone theme is now heard on top in the tromba.*
- *b56 – part of the ritornello theme now played by the cello/violone, while the soloists and upper ripieno strings accompany.*

However, the soloists have their own separate themes, which only they play (bb84-11 violin, bb32-35 tromba and oboe in imitation). The soloists also have passages where they are accompanied only by the continuo, allowing the recorder in particular to be heard more clearly e.g. bb17-18. This is also typical of the contrasting solo and tutti passages heard in a concerto grosso.[13]

The 2nd movement provides a striking contrast to the 1st in that the ripieno and tromba are silent, leaving a 3-part polyphonic texture accompanied by the continuo. This is more a chamber movement than an orchestral one.[14]

The tromba returns to announce the 3rd movement,[15] and the other soloists gradually enter in a fugal exposition (b7 oboe, b21 violin, b27 recorder), but the ripieno are still silent. At

---

[10] This question is about texture and the different roles played by sections of Bach's orchestra. Be sure to focus on this aspect in your answer; other areas are irrelevant here.

[11] The candidate briefly clarifies the question and demonstrates good knowledge of the scoring.

[12] Remember bullet points are perfectly acceptable in an answer on this paper, and they serve here as a good way of organizing multiple examples.

[13] Good awareness of the significance of the textures used by Bach.

[14] There is not much to say here about the 2nd movement, but a brief reference is required by the question.

[15] This question lends itself well to a chronological approach when planning an answer. Be on the lookout for opportunities to use this method.

one point the continuo fall silent as well (bb41-46) leaving the soloists briefly as an ensemble in their own right. The ripieno and continuo enter together at b47, but their role here is more to accompany the soloists in detached homophonic chords (bb47-52).

From here to the end the upper ripieno strings alternate between silence and tutti passages where they accompany the other instruments (b97, simple sustained harmony), so their role is somewhat reduced compared with the 1st movement.[16] However the cello and violone do share melodic material with the soloists e.g. bb79-85, where they are in imitation with the tromba and recorder. The soloists also accompany occasionally (bb122-125 detached chords for tromba, recorder and oboe) but mostly they are in counterpoint with each other.

Although the relationship between the soloists and the ripieno upper strings[17] does change after the 1st movement, the cello and violone continue to regularly share in the melodic material in counterpoint with the soloists throughout most of the piece. This final point makes Brandenburg Concerto no. 2 a good example of the polarized texture (florid melodies, purposeful bass, and harmonic filling from continuo and ripieno) which was such a prominent feature of the Baroque style.[18]

Here is an answer to Question 3 from the Musical Links practice questions, again written under timed conditions. Here, the candidate has used detailed bullet points based on and developing the outlines given in the tables starting on **page 74**. You could decide to present your answer as a table, but remember to flesh out the outlines with a more detailed explanation of what is happening in both scores.

Investigate significant musical links between the two prescribed works by comparing and contrasting their use of form and structure.

Answer:

There are a number of structural links that can be made between Bach's Brandenburg Concerto no. 2 (BC2) and Kodály's Dances of Galánta *(DoG):[19]*

- *Both works employ a recurring theme, which in Bach's time would been called Ritornello form. A principal ritornello theme would reappear between other episodes of music, often*

---

[16] Good observation in response to the question!

[17] Well clarified; there is a distinction to be made between the roles of the upper and lower ripieno strings.

[18] Again, good awareness of the significance of the textures used in a wider context.

[19] A good time-saving tip is to abbreviate the long titles of both pieces; the candidate has clearly stated their intention to do so in the introduction.

in a shortened form and in different related keys.[20] *BC2 1st movement fits this model well, as can be seen below:*

- ○ *Complete 8-bar ritornello theme in tonic key F major*[21] *bb04-8*
- ○ *bb23-28 – now in Dominant key C major and 2 bars shorter*
- ○ *bb56-59 – now in Subdominant key Bb major and only 4 bars long*

- *A similar model can also be seen in DoG, with the 1st Dance acting like a ritornello theme, although here the range of tonality is much greater:*
  - ○ *bb50-65 – 16 bars, starting in (dominant) E minor*
  - ○ *bb151-167 – also 16 bars, starting in (tonic) A minor*
  - ○ *bb229-232 – only 4 bars, but now in the more distant Lydian dominant scale on Bb (with a raised 4th E♮)*[22]

- *Both works also make use of multiple forms within their overall structure:*
  - ○ *BC2 3rd movement begins with a fugue bb1-46 in F major. Exposition bb1-32, episode bb33-40, and a middle entry bb41-46. This leads straight into a ritornello structure starting at b47 and running to the end with alternate tutti and solo passages in the concerto grosso style.*[23]
  - ○ *DoG has an over-arching Hungarian 'verbunkos' structure (slow bb1-235, fast bb236-607). Within the slow section, there is a fantasia-like introduction bb1-49, and the aforementioned*[24] *ritornello form from b50. Each of the dances themselves are usually in Binary form AABB, with repeated phrases (e.g. 2nd Dance: A bb96 and 103 flute; B bb109 and 133 clarinet/strings and flute), typical of many folk dances around the world.*[25]

- *Both works use themes or motifs to help unify the piece as a whole:*
  - ○ *BC2: the 2nd movement has a motif F-F-E (bb33-41 violin) which is heard earlier in the 1st movement (bb634-641 recorder Bb-Bb-Ab, repeated in a descending sequence)*
  - ○ *DoG: the 1st Dance ritornello theme already mentioned, returns much later in the coda near the end (b567). Furthermore the syncopated*[26] *falling octave motif used frequently in the 5th Dance b443 onwards, was first heard in the poco meno mosso melody at b363 (1st violin). Such motifs were also an important feature of the fast section in a verbunkos dance.*

---

[20] A brief description of ritornello is useful here to support the links argument.

[21] Remember that many structures are linked to tonality, so it is important to include this information.

[22] Good mention of a difference in amongst the similarities.

[23] A detailed but concise explanation of the chosen example.

[24] There is no need to rewrite the example here; simply refer to it in your answer.

[25] Good comment, relating the example to a wider context.

[26] This could perhaps be notated (♪♩ ♪).

Section B

1. *Byrd – Ave verum corpus (score included)*

Musical Features:
Four unaccompanied choral parts; G minor, slow tempo in 4/4 time; frequent suspensions e.g. bb3-4 soprano and tenor; *tierce de Picardie* b4; false relation b2 (soprano F#, bass F♮); regular cadences, imperfect in G minor bb7-8 and bb14-15, perfect in B flat major bb21-22; homophonic texture with some independent parts bb1-7; antiphony between soprano and alto/tenor/bass bb28-31; imitation bb31-35 (*O Jesu Fili*).

Structure:
Through-composed bb1-28; Byrd introduces new musical ideas for each phrase of the words.
Repeat mark at b29 shows a reprise of the music beyond the end of the given extract.

Context:
Motet in Latin, sung during a Christian church service, English, Renaissance 1590s or early 1600s.

2. *Shostakovich – Symphony no. 7 1st movement 'Invasion theme' (score not included)*

Musical Features:
Allegro, 4/4, strict march-like tempo; military-style side drum ostinato rhythm throughout; main theme built from 2-bar phrases, featuring a dotted rhythm and played with detached accents on most notes; dynamics become louder with each new presentation of the theme; major key confirmed by ostinato bass/accompaniment centred on the tonic; dissonance caused by parallel major triads.

Structure:
Main theme heard four times in a series of orchestral variations:
0'00" clarinet (high tessitura) in canon with oboe/cor anglais
0'46" upper strings in parallel major chords
1'24" upper woodwinds join in with the parallel major chords
2'03" theme in lower brass (trombones/tuba) with a new ostinato in xylophone/woodwind

Context:
From a symphony for large orchestra performed in a concert hall. 20th century (1941) due to the parallel major triads and ostinati. Shostakovich

named his *Symphony no. 7* 'Leningrad' in tribute to the Soviet citizens who lost their lives in World War II.

3. *Schumann – Piano Quartet 3rd movement (score not included)*

Musical Features:
Adagio, 3/4, major key; violin, viola, cello and piano; melody features some wide expressive leaps; falling chromatic scale at the end of the melody; 4-bar phrases in descending sequence; chordal piano accompaniment; diatonic harmony with visits to related minor keys and some chromatic chords; calm, legato playing style.

Structure:
0'00" a brief introduction starting with a diminished 7th chord
0'11" lyrical melody in the cello
0'50" violin takes over the melody, imitation in the cello
1'29" piano has a new syncopated melody over the same harmony as the earlier sections, with viola counter-melodies
2'17" music changes key and moves into a new section

Context:
Nineteenth-century Romantic chamber music, the slow movement of a piano quartet in 4 movements, written in 1842. For performance in a drawing/living room for the pleasure of the performers themselves and possibly a small audience.

4. *Beethoven – Symphony no. 7 2nd movement (score included)*

Musical Features:
Allegretto in 2/4 time; main theme in A minor, modulates to relative major (C) before returning to tonic; simple theme built from crotchets and quavers in repeated notes and conjunct movement; regular 4-bar phrases; texture and dynamics gradually build up from *p* lower strings to a *ff* tutti; polyrhythm in 2nd violins/violas/cellos from 2'11" (quavers/quaver triplets); sequence at 0'19" using major/minor triads; counter-melody features short glissandi and some descending chromatic movement.

Structure:
0'00" single tonic chord (woodwind/french horns)
0'05" simple 16-bar theme in violas; 2nd half repeated *pp*
0'47" theme in 2nd violins, counter-melody in violas/cellos

1'30" theme in 1st violins, counter-melody in 2nd violins, arpeggio accompaniment in lower strings; gradual crescendo

2'11" tutti, with theme in woodwinds/horns, counter-melody now an octave higher in 1st violins

Context:
Late Classical period (1811–12). This is the slow movement (despite the Allegretto tempo the metronome marking is only 76) of a 4-movement symphony for orchestra intended for performance in a concert hall. The movement was encored at its first performance in Vienna and has been popular ever since. Beethoven himself thought the *7th Symphony* was one of his best works.

5. *Handel – Messiah no. 14–17 (score not included)*

Musical Features:
Recitative 0'00": soprano solo, speech rhythms, flexible tempo dictated by the words, pedal point in the cello, spread chords in the harpsichord, appoggiatura 0'10".

Accompanied recitative 0'13": in tempo, with cello and harpsichord continuo and violin arpeggios, perfect cadence at the end.

Chorus: major key, 4/4, SATB chorus accompanied by strings, continuo and Baroque high-pitched trumpet. Contrasting music for each line of words: 1'23" homophonic, dotted rhythms for upper voices, with busy violin passage work; 1'33" longer rhythms in octaves for lower voices/instruments; 1'59" chorus parts enter in the order BTAS as the polyphonic texture builds.

Structure:
0'00" recitative (continuo accompaniment)
0'13" accompanied recitative
0'33" recitative, continuo, change of key, moves from major to minor
1'08" accompanied recitative, segue straight into […]
1'23" chorus, two contrasting ideas
1'59" new imitative melody
2'15" reprise of chorus opening from 1'23"

Context:
Late Baroque oratorio, sung in English, written for performance in a concert hall, church or theatre. The very first oratorios were produced for an opera house during Christian festivals such as Lent, when staging operas

was forbidden. Handel's *Messiah* was composed in 1741, and this dramatic sequence of recitatives and a chorus telling part of the Christmas story helped to establish it as one of the best-known choral works in Western art music.

6. *Nat Adderley – Work Song (score not included)*

Musical Features:
Fast 4/4; muted trumpet/cornet, guitar, double bass (plucked), drums, piano; imitation between muted trumpet and double bass/guitar from the start; string/note bends on guitar/bass 0'12"; main theme uses blues scale; blue notes e.g. flattened 5th 0'19"-0'23"; solos accompanied by swing rhythm on drums, walking bass, syncopated chords on guitar/piano; harmony centred on tonic/dominant chords; chords often have additional notes/extensions.

Structure:
Head arrangement, with chorus (16 bars, 4 x 4-bar phrases) and a series of solos based on the chord pattern/changes.
0'00" chorus
0'26" repeat of chorus
0'51" trumpet solo 1
1'15" trumpet solo 2
1'39" guitar solo

Context:
American 5-piece jazz group recording live together in a studio, part of an album for commercial release, and promoted with touring and media appearances. The album (of which this is the title track) was recorded in 1960 in what became known as the hard bop style, a sub-genre of bebop with more Blues influences.

7. *Africando – Betece (score not included)*

Musical Features:
Minor key, harmony uses the primary triads (I, IV and V) throughout; piano, acoustic guitar, trumpets, trombones, baritone saxophone, bass guitar, percussion including bongos, cowbell, snare drum with brushes, guiro, congas, timbales, male voices; moderate 4/4 with several layers of different syncopated ostinato rhythms; Cuban-style piano with hands 2 octaves apart; call and response between guitar and other pitched instruments 0'17"; chorus and instrumental phrases sung/played in parallel 3rds.

Structure:
0'00" introduction – piano first, followed by brass at 0'05"
0'17" link passage (precedes each chorus)
0'28" chorus (with brass fills between the vocal lines)
0'44" verse 1 (solo)
1'09" link passage
1'19" chorus as before
1'34" verse 2
1'50" guitar solo (played in octaves)

Context:
Culturally this song is not as easy to place as you might think; it is in fact African Salsa, a fusion of Latin American and African elements from a band originally formed in New York! However, credit would still be given for (rightly) identifying any of the features above as Latin American. Recorded in a studio in 2000 for commercial release and also intended for dancing.

8. *Yu Cheng – Springtime on the Tianshan Mountains (score not included)*

Musical Features:
Pipa (a 4-stringed instrument plucked like a lute), bamboo flute, accompanied by erhu, shaker/tambourine and a drum; tremolo picking sustains the longer notes of the melody; drone on the tonic and dominant throughout; 0'19" melody starts on the dominant; melody mostly on the natural minor scale (Aeolian mode) except for the dissonance at 1'21", which is caused by a flattened supertonic (2nd degree of the scale just above the tonic); bamboo flute answers the pipa phrases with a short imitation e.g. 0'48", and in the faster section has a greater share of the melody; call and response 1'38" and 1'51".

Structure:
Two contrasting main sections suggesting a binary form:
0'00" introduction establishes the drone
0'19" slow melody, free flexible tempo
0'57" slow melody repeated, but louder
1'36" faster melody in a stricter 3/4 time, with repeated phrases
Context:
Traditional Chinese folk music to be played and danced to at the imperial court, quite possibly dating back well over a thousand years. Cheng Yu is an internationally renowned scholar and virtuoso of Chinese music.

9. *LeMoyne-Owen College – Chikuyu (score not included)*

Musical Features:

Moderate tempo in 4/4; talking drum, marimba, djembes, shakers, dun dun (a low-pitched drum giving the pulse); 1st melody has a tremolo on the first note (a roll with two mallets) then a falling figure; 2nd melody has repeating 2-bar question and answer phrases – 1st phrase is a conjunct syncopated idea, the 2nd phrase is similar but starts a fifth lower; melody based on the Phrygian mode; drum accompaniment is several layers of different ostinato rhythms (polyrhythm).

Structure:

0'00" short talking drum introduction with rising pitch bends
0'02" 1st marimba melody
0'20" 2nd marimba melody
0'39" shaker enters with a dotted rhythm
1'35" 1st melody returns, another shaker enters

Context:

Performed by the LeMoyne-Owen College African Drumming Ensemble (LOCADE), this is a recent recording made for commercial release. The origins of the piece are unclear, but based on an African music tradition intended for dancing and ceremonial purposes. Chikuyu is a small neighbourhood in Tanzania.

INDEX